A Teaching Assistant's Guide to Child Development and Psychology in the Classroom

Teaching assistants play a vital role in today's schools. This book will help them to get to grips with the main issues to do with psychology and its role in the processes of teaching and learning.

The author provides informative yet down-to-earth commentary on the basic principles underlying children's development and addresses issues such as:

- How to support learning
- What are the basic learning styles?
- Teaching children with special educational needs
- How to deal with disruptive behaviour
- How to help children with their self-esteem and independence

Chapters are complemented throughout with lively case studies, and guidance on using reflection in the classroom, to help readers critically review their own professional practice.

This book covers the relevant knowledge base requirements at both NVQ/SVQ level 2 and 3 which relates to psychology and education as outlined in the National Occupational Standards and will also be an invaluable aid for all teaching assistants in schools.

Susan Bentham is Head of Psychology at Bognor Regis Adult Education Centre.

D0170206

A Teaching Assistant's Guide to Child Development and Psychology in the Classroom

Susan Bentham

RoutledgeFalmer
Taylor & Francis Group

LONDON AND NEW YORK

First published 2004
by RoutledgeFalmer
11 New Fetter Lane, London EC4P 4EE

Simultaneously published in the USA and Canada
by RoutledgeFalmer
29 West 35th Street, New York, NY 10001

RoutledgeFalmer is an imprint of the Taylor & Francis Group

© 2004 Susan Bentham

Typeset in Bembo and Gill by BC Typesetting, Bristol
Printed and bound in Great Britain by
TJ International Ltd, Padstow, Cornwall

British Library Cataloguing in Publication Data
A catalogue record for this book is available from the British Library

Library of Congress Cataloging in Publication Data
A catalog record has been requested

ISBN 0-415-31108-X (pbk)
ISBN 0-415-31107-1 (hbk)

To the teaching assistants who have inspired
this book

Contents

List of tables

Acknowledgements

Susan Bentham would like to thank all her students, past and present. This book would not have been possible without them. Maria Cumbers, Jane Benham, Jackie Martin, Carole Hillier, Amanda Harris, Lynne Fowler, Catherine Harper, Frances Bayliss, Julie Gibbs, Nicky Searle, Victoria Gambling, Dawn Hoar.

Introduction

This book was inspired by and written for teaching assistants. The book can be used on several levels.

On a general level, this book aims to give readers an understanding of basic concepts relating to child development and psychology. Knowledge of such issues is interesting, but what the teaching assistants that I have worked with want to know is how they can use this information in the classroom to better support the students they work with. This book will give many examples of how the theories and concepts can both explain student behaviour and be used to support learning. Above all this book aims to be reader-friendly, practical and hands-on. However, in explaining the concepts of child development and psychology there is a lot of terminology. Whenever new terminology first occurs in this book it will be highlighted in bold type. New terminology will be explained within the text. In addition, definitions of key concepts can be found in the glossary at the back of the book. Terminology can seem overwhelming at first, but a grasp of such terms can help teaching assistants communicate more effectively with other teaching professionals.

Another feature of this book will be its emphasis on reflection. Each chapter of the book will finish with a reflective component. The reflective component will consist of a short story describing some event which a teaching assistant has experienced in the course of a day. As the reader you will be asked to imagine what you would do if you were that teaching assistant and to consider how the knowledge presented in the book would help you in both understanding and dealing with the event. There is much more to be said on reflection, but that we will come to in a moment.

On a very specific level this book was written in view of the National Occupational Standards for teaching assistants. Many new courses for teaching assistants are being developed in line with these standards at both NVQ Level 2 and 3. This book aims to cover many of the knowledge requirements for these new courses. A matrix at the back of the book maps the chapters on to the National Occupational Standards.

Some courses following these standards will ask for performance evidence in the form of reflective journals, personal accounts or case studies. In these cases, the reflective component, at the end of each chapter, will help you, the teaching assistant, to write and comment about everyday events. Discussing the reflective components can also be used as an effective teaching tool on such courses.

The next section defines reflection and outlines examples of how to reflect. A reading of this section will give the reader an understanding of the value of reflection and a practical way of reflecting.

Definitions of reflection

'Reflection' is a word that is often used in the field of education. Teachers as part of their role are encouraged to be reflective practitioners. But what is reflection and what is a reflective practitioner? And more to the point, as this book is for teaching assistants how does reflection relate to what teaching assistants do on a daily basis?

Reflection has been defined as a 'kind of thinking that consists in turning a subject over in the mind and giving it serious thought' (Dewey 1933). The subject in this case is your working day. At the end of a working day you might want to go home, put your feet up, enjoy a soothing drink of your choice and forget. But perhaps your mind can't switch off and your thoughts wander back to something that happened at school, some incident that went really well or perhaps something that did not go quite as you had hoped. Reflection starts with replaying an event in your mind. The purpose of replaying the event is to try to understand or make sense of what happened. Sometimes in order to understand or make sense of what happened thinking is not enough. Sometimes you need to talk to others about what happened. You might need to ask for advice. You might need to seek more information. This is all part of reflection. The hope is that through reflection, that is, through seriously thinking about what you do and how you do it you will become better at what you do. When you start to think about how you do what you do on a regular basis you are well on your way to becoming a reflective practitioner.

The use of reflective practice as a way of improving teaching assistants' professional skills

Reflection sounds interesting but how do you start? First it is helpful to write your thoughts down. This can take the form of a diary or a personal account. When describing what happened it is helpful to structure your thoughts. One way of writing down your thoughts has been devised by Gibbs (1988, p. 52) who talks of a reflective cycle. This cycle is as follows:

- *Description.* Here as the name implies you state what happened. Sometimes it may be helpful to write down what should have happened.
- *Feelings.* What were you thinking and feeling? Perhaps you could also add how you thought the students were thinking and feeling? It might be helpful to consider how confident you felt in the situation.
- *Evaluation.* What was difficult about the event? What was good about the event? It is important to realise that evaluation is not always negative. If a lesson with a student has gone really well then you will want to know what it was that made that lesson effective so you can use that approach again. However, it is also true that sometimes in life we actually learn more when things don't go the way we had planned.
- *Analysis.* How do you make sense of what has happened? Why do you think this happened? Has anything similar happened to you before? Can any psychological theories explain what happened? As you find out more about psychology and child development you will be able to use this information to help you to reflect.
- *In conclusion.* What else could you have done?
- *Action plan.* If the event occurs again what would you do differently? What can you do to feel more confident in such situations?

This is a cycle as there is never an end to reflection. The action plan leads on to the next event, which leads to the next cycle of questioning. At this point you might be saying that this seems too much like hard work and that you don't often think about what you do, you just do it. In the next section we will look at two specific case studies and how this model of reflection or questioning can be applied to these case studies.

Examples of how to reflect using reflective journals

Case study 1

Wendy, a teaching assistant in a primary school, was on playground duty. Wendy describes the following incident. 'I noticed James playing on the grass area behind the fence. As it is an out of bounds area, I went up to James and asked him to leave the area and come back with me to the playground. He refused to leave. He shouted: "I don't have to do what you say!" I took his hand and expected him to come with me, but he then fell to the ground and started making faces. I asked him again to come back to the playground and he told me to f*** off. Another child that I knew was near by and I asked that child to go and tell the Deputy Head, who was also on playground duty, what was happening. I tried again to coax him back into the playground, but now he started screaming. Mrs Murphy the Deputy Head arrived at this point and thanked me for my involvement and told me to go back to the playground. Miss Murphy told James very firmly that she had had enough of his nonsense and to get up and to go back with her. James got up and went into the playground with Miss Murphy.'

Example of workplace journal

Name

Wendy Lawson.

Description of event (What happened? What should have happened?)

I was on playground duty. One child was in the out of bounds area. When I asked him to leave, he refused, fell to the ground and was abusive. I asked another child to go and fetch the Deputy Head. She thanked me for my involvement and quickly dealt with the child.

Feelings (What did I feel? What did I think the student felt?)

I know I did the right thing in calling for assistance, but I felt that I should have really been able to cope with the situation by myself. Even though I have been working in the school for over a year now, I still don't always feel confident in dealing with children who are disruptive. As for James, well, he was very upset. I just don't know what got into him, as he is usually a co-operative child.

Evaluation (What was good? What was difficult?)

What was good about the event was that the situation was sorted and that the Deputy Head brought James back into the school grounds. It was good that I took action to get back-up from the Deputy Head. What was difficult about the event? Well, I feel maybe if I had acted differently I would have been able to handle the situation.

Analysis (How do I make sense of this? Why did this happen?)

I don't know why James behaved in this manner.

In conclusion (What else could I have done?)

What else could I have done? Well, I actually spent a lot of time thinking about this. In the end I felt I was going nowhere so I decided to talk to my friend Sheila, who is also a teaching assistant. Sheila has been at the school for over five years. She suggested that maybe I should have asked him why he was in the out of bounds area in the first place. I never thought to ask him that. Sheila said that she had noticed that earlier there had seemed to be some sort of fight between James and his best friend Sam. Perhaps if I had asked James why he was there, he might not have thrown himself down on the ground. Sheila also suggested that I go to the Deputy Head and ask her for her advice. Maybe the Deputy Head has some tips on behaviour management.

Action plan (Next time I would . . .)

What would I do next time? Well, that is hard to say. Perhaps keep an extra eye on that area and actually remind students who are getting too close to the area that they need to move somewhere else rather than wait till they are out of bounds and then have to tell them off. What can I do to feel more confident? That is a very difficult question. The Deputy Head has offered to find me some handouts on managing disruptive behaviour. That might help. But what has helped my confidence has been talking about this to Sheila and the Deputy Head. The Deputy Head was very supportive in that I had done the right thing.

Self-assessment

The above example outlines how Wendy made sense of the event.

1   How would you make sense of the event?
2   Can you think of any other explanations for James's behaviour?
3   Can you think of any other ways to deal with James's behaviour?

Case study 2

Chris was a teaching assistant in a large secondary school. Chris was working in a Year 8 history class playing a game with seven students. The game was a sort of Trivial Pursuit game that tested their knowledge on key facts that they would need to know for their upcoming test. At the end of the session Chris reported: 'Well, on the whole I think it went very well, though there were a few problems at the beginning. There was an argument between these two lads about who was to start first and it took a while to sort that out. In the end I decided who was going to start. However, the game went well and most of the students asked if they could play the game next lesson, so they must have really enjoyed it. Though maybe not all of the students enjoyed it as two of them wandered off to do something else.'

Example of workplace journal

Name

Chris Keen.

Description of event (What happened? What should have happened?)

My task as set out by the teacher was to play a revision game. The teacher told me what students I would be working with and for the entire session we played the game.

Feelings (What did I feel? What did the student/students feel?)

I think that it was a very enjoyable and useful session. I felt that the session went well. The students must have enjoyed the session, as they wanted to play it again. However, two students did wander off to do something else, so maybe they didn't enjoy the game. On the whole I felt very confident.

Evaluation (What was good? What was difficult?)

What was good about the session? Well, the game really involved them in learning. They were revising the key facts but it didn't feel like revising, as it was a game. What was difficult about the session? Well, there was some time wasted at the beginning as two students were arguing about who went first and of course two students did wander off.

Analysis (How do I make sense of this? Why did this happen?)

On the whole I think that having the students actively involved in learning by playing the game made for a good learning session. I don't know why two students left half-way through the game.

Conclusion (What else could I have done?)

What else could I have done? Well, I think I should have had a clear plan about who should have started first. For instance whoever throws the highest on the dice. As it was I just simply asked who wants to start first and that just started the argument. As to the two students who wandered off, I went up to them later and asked why. They just shrugged their shoulders and said it was boring. But I was wondering if maybe some of the questions were just too difficult for them and they just didn't want to be shown up in front of their friends.

Action plan (Next time I would . . .)

What would I do next time? Well, I think I would definitely have a range of questions to ask, starting with some easy ones.

Self-assessment

The above example outlines how Chris made sense of the event.

1   How would you make sense of the event?
2   Can you think of any other explanations for why the students wandered off from the game?

3 Can you think of any other ways to deal with the students' behaviour?

Final comments

If you have done the self-assessment questions you will have probably come up with alternative reasons for why James was in the out of bounds area or why Chris's students wandered off from the revision game. You might have come up with other ideas or ways to deal with James or how to keep Chris's students interested in the history game. There is no one right answer. Reflection involves coming up with possible ideas that will keep students on track and ideas that will enable them to learn more effectively. Reflection involves experimentation, that is, trying out these ideas and seeing what works. Reflection also involves talking over your ideas with others especially the teacher.

Reflection is not easy! Reflection requires serious thinking. But hopefully what these examples and your own consideration of these events has shown is that thinking or reflecting about situations leads to a greater understanding of the situation and ideas about how to become better at what you do.

Chapter 1

Basic principles underlying pupil development and learning

This chapter outlines how individuals develop and learn. We know from experience that there is a world of a difference between what a three-year-old can do compared with a thirteen-year-old. The big question that various theorists have attempted to explain is how this change occurs.

Many theorists talk about stages of development, that is, they outline what the average child can do at a certain age and how the behaviour of this average child changes through time. Now while this approach is useful in suggesting what to expect at certain ages, we also know that even children of the same age can differ widely in terms of what they can and cannot do. In fact there is no such animal as the average child. However, if a child is behaving in a manner that is considerably different from what we would expect, then this could indicate some underlying issue. (For further discussion see Chapter 4.)

What we will also discover is that different theorists have different views. But if debate exists, you might want to ask what is the right view? There is no *one* right view, as all theories offer some insights into how individuals develop and learn. The fact that debate exists highlights the complexity of learning and development.

Intellectual and cognitive skills

Piaget

In common day language when we say someone is intellectual we are saying that we think they are very clever or smart. But what do we mean by clever? In part intellectual ability is due to cognitive skills, that is, how someone thinks and reasons through ideas and problems.

Jean Piaget (1896–1980) devoted his adult life to the study of **cognitive development**, that is, how individuals learn to think and how thinking develops over time. Piaget was interested in tracking how thinking develops from a newborn infant, through the terrible twos, to the student just beginning school, to the lanky adolescent and finally onwards to the emerging adult. Piaget studied thinking by observing children doing specific tasks and by asking them specific questions. For example, Piaget was interested in how children came to understand why some objects float in water, while others sink. Piaget was interested in how children would solve such problems as: 'if Amy is taller than Susan and Sarah is shorter than Susan. Who is the taller, Amy or Sarah?'

One of Piaget's greatest insights started with the awareness that a child's manner of thinking is very different from that of an adult and that thinking changes with time. Thinking changes not only quantitatively but also qualitatively. Quantitatively refers to the amount of thinking, while qualitatively refers to the style or manner in which we think.

Cognitive development according to Piaget was due to an interaction between the developing individual and the individual's experience within the environment. Piaget believed that children were little scientists who constructed or created knowledge by being actively involved in what was going on around them. Children learned best by discovering things for themselves. However, what children can learn is limited by their age. A thirteen-year-old can be taught algebra, but a two-year-old can't. Children of four or five can begin to learn to read. But can you teach an eighteen-month-old child to read? Piaget labelled this as **maturational readiness**. At a certain age a child's thinking ability develops to a point that makes it possible for a child to learn certain skills. Obviously this has important implications for when certain skills are taught in schools. Piaget went on further to describe how individuals learn new information. Central to Piaget's theory is the concept of **schemas**. Schemas are units of mental thought. Schemas have been compared to files in which we store information. But how do schemas develop in the first place? To answer this question Piaget outlined a process called **adaptation**, which involved **assimilation** and **accommodation**. This sounds quite complex but the following case study illustrates how this terminology can relate to everyday experiences.

Case study 1.1

Imagine a primary maths classroom. The teaching assistant is working with two students (Sam and Kylie) on shape, in particular the difference between squares and rectangles. Each child has in front of them ten shapes, five squares and five rectangles of varying size and colour. The task is to sort the shapes into piles of squares and rectangles.

Kylie knows that squares have four sides and so have rectangles, but squares are different from rectangles in that all four sides are the same length. Kylie looks at all the shapes and is a little bit confused by the fact that some shapes are bigger than others, but Kylie remembers that for a shape to be a square it must have four sides of equal length, so it does not matter if some squares are bigger than others. On the other hand Kylie also knows that rectangles do not have sides of equal length. Kylie correctly sorts the shapes into squares and rectangles. She has taken this new information regarding different sizes of squares and rectangles and fitted it, or assimilated it, into her existing understanding of what squares and rectangles are.

Sam has problems with this task. He quickly sorts the shapes out into two piles corresponding to big shapes and small shapes. The teaching assistant asks him where are the squares. Sam says all the shapes are squares. The teaching assistant asks him where are the rectangles. Sam says all the shapes are rectangles. Sam says all the shapes are the same because they have four corners. The teaching assistant tries to explain that there is a difference between squares and rectangles. Sam looks upset as he realises he has got it wrong. Here Sam has an existing schema about shape that states squares and rectangles are the same as they have four corners. Sam is correct but there are also differences between squares and rectangles. Sam's understanding of squares and rectangles is not the same as society's shared understanding of what is a square and what is a rectangle. Sam is experiencing what Piaget would term **cognitive disequilibrium**. Sam realises sadly that how he understands squares and rectangles is not the same as everyone else. According to Piaget this state of cognitive disequilibrium is unpleasant and that will motivate Sam to try to figure out the difference between a square and a rectangle. Sam needs to create a new schema for squares and rectangles. The process of creating new schemas is called 'accommodation.

To summarise:

- Schemas are units of mental thought.
- Adaptation explains the process of learning.
- Adaptation involves both assimilation and accommodation.
- Assimilation is when you take new information and fit it into an existing schema or file.
- When new experiences cannot fit into existing schemas or files then an unpleasant state of cognitive disequilibrium is said to exist.
- In order to put an end to this state of cognitive disequilibrium, the individual must create new schemas, through a process called accommodation.

Piaget believed that cognitive development occurred in four stages. These stages were universal as everyone went through these stages in the same order and at no time could an individual skip or miss stages. Though Piaget stated corresponding ages for various stages, he did note that there could be variation, that is, some children would enter the stage earlier and some children would enter the stage later. Piaget's stages are as follows:

Sensori-motor stage (birth to two years)

The achievements of this stage are **object permanence** and **general symbolic function**. Object permanence is the awareness that something exists in time and space even if we cannot see it. For example, does a young child realise that teddy still exists even if teddy is put away in the toybox. The classic test for this is to fully cover a toy with a cloth while a baby is watching. The important part is that the baby sees you hide the toy. Will the baby search and find the toy or will the baby act as though 'out of sight is out of mind'. Surprisingly it is not until eight to twelve months that a baby will actively search for and find a toy that they have seen being hidden. General symbolic function includes the emergence of language, make-believe play and **deferred imitation**. Deferred imitation is an important skill, which starts with watching someone else; in particular watching what a person does and noting exactly what happens to that person. Deferred imitation then involves deliberating or thinking about whether the behaviour viewed was worth repeating. If the behaviour was seen as worthwhile, the individual waits and when an opportunity arises remembers the initial behaviour and then copies that behaviour. For example John is twenty months and is an only child. When John is good his mother gives him a chocolate biscuit, which she keeps in a cupboard well out of his reach. One day John's three-year-old cousin comes to visit. John's mom gives them both biscuits. While the mothers are busy in another room talking John watches as his cousin goes into the kitchen, moves a chair, climbs on to the chair and then on to the counter and opens the cupboard and gets another biscuit. The next day John's mother walks into the kitchen to find John standing on the counter eating a chocolate biscuit. This according to Piaget is an example of deferred imitation.

Pre-operational stage (two to seven years)

This stage sees an amazing growth in the use of language and the beginnings of problem solving. Children begin to develop concepts such as: How many? How much does it weigh? How tall is it? What time is it? However, children at this age are limited in their logical thinking as according to Piaget they are egocentric and unable to **decentre**. **Egocentrism**, or being egocentric, involves the child believing that others see the world as they do. The classic test for this is known as the three mountains test. The test goes like this:

1 The child is shown a three-dimensional model of three mountains; one with snow on it, one with a cabin on it and the last mountain with a cross on it. The child sits at one end of the table while a doll is placed at the other end.
2 The child is then shown a series of pictures of the mountains taken from different perspectives.
3 The child is asked to select what picture best represents what they see and what picture best represents what the doll sees.

In order to do this task the child needs to realise that what they see is different from what the doll sees as they are looking at the mountains from different angles. In addition the child needs to visualise in their mind what the doll sees from the doll's position. This is a difficult test and it is not until nine that a child can accurately select the view that the doll sees.

When a child has the ability to see the world from another's perspective Piaget would say they have the ability to decentre. To decentre involves the child holding and understanding two apparently opposing views in their mind at the same time. In the three mountains test a child has decentred when they realise that what the doll sees is different from what they see because the doll is at the other end of the table.

Piaget was also interested in children's ability to **conserve**. Conservation involves the realisation that an object remains the same even though its appearance changes. Piaget developed many tests to explore children's understanding of conservation. The conservation of number test goes like this:

EXPERIMENTER (shows two identical lines of beads): Do the two rows have the same number of beads?

● ● ● ● ●

● ● ● ● ●

FIVE-YEAR-OLD CHILD: Yes.
EXPERIMENTER (rearranges one row by increasing the spaces between the beads): Do the two rows have the same number of beads?

● ● ● ● ●

● ● ● ● ●

FIVE-YEAR-OLD CHILD: That row has more! (Pointing to the row with the greater spaces between the beads.)

Here the child has been fooled by appearances; the row looks longer so therefore it must have more. The child's failure to conserve can be explained by their inability to decentre, that is, their inability to hold in their mind two apparently opposing views. It is not until age six that a child will be able to reason that though the rows look different nothing has changed. A six-year-old child might say that: 'The rows are the same, they just look different. They still have the same number. You just moved them.'

Concrete operational stage (seven to eleven years)

Children at this stage are better at logical thinking. Children can now successfully answer questions relating to **transitivity**, a type of reasoning, which is illustrated in the following: 'If Amy is taller than Susan and Sarah is shorter than Susan. Who is the taller, Amy or Sarah?'

However, children in this stage are limited in regard to their logical thinking as they can only think about things that are actually present. An example to illustrate this point would involve asking children the question: 'If you had a third eye where would you put it and why?' Typically children in this stage will place the third eye in the middle of their forehead between their existing eyes. Here the children are bound by the realities of the world, that eyes are located on a certain part of your face (Sigelman and Shaffer 1991). It is not until age eleven or twelve that children develop the skill of abstract thinking and can consider possibilities that contradict reality.

Formal operational stage (eleven to twelve years and over)

This is the stage that children have developed the beginnings of abstract thought. It is for this reason that algebra is not taught until a child is eleven or twelve. Individuals of this age now engage in what is termed **hypothetical deductive reasoning**. This involves generating a hypothesis, stating the implications of the hypothesis, testing the hypothesis, drawing conclusions and finally generating or coming up with yet more hypotheses.

To summarise

For Piaget, cognitive development was due to an interaction between the developing child and the child's experience within the environment. Piaget stated that the newly acquired knowledge was stored in the form of schemas, units of mental thought. Schemas were in turn formed through the processes of assimilation and accommodation. Piaget believed that children progressed through four stages of cognitive development. The first stage, sensori–motor (birth to two years) was characterised by the development of object permanence, language, make-believe play and deferred imitation. In the next stage, pre-operational (two to seven), the child's thinking lacked logic, and the child could be fooled by the ways things looked, i.e. if it looked like it was bigger, then it must be bigger. The child also had difficulty in stating how what they saw was different from what other people would see. This was illustrated in Piaget's three mountains test. In the next stage, concrete operations (seven to eleven years), the child could use logic, but only on objects that were actually present. The final stage, formal operations (eleven to twelve or more years), saw the development of abstract thought.

Vygotsky

Vygotsky was a Russian theorist who wrote on education, sociology, art, history and philosophy. Though Vygotsky died in 1933, his views on education are very influential today. Vygotsky emphasised the importance of social interactions in cognitive development. If we remember Piaget saw children as young scientists discovering knowledge for themselves through being actively involved in the world around them. Vygotsky stated that being actively involved was not enough, but that for learning to happen, children need to be engaged in talking with others about what they were supposed to be learning and that specifically they needed support and guidance from someone more experienced in regard to how to learn.

One of Vygotsky's key ideas concerned what he termed the **Zone of Proximal Development** (ZPD). The Zone of Proximal Development outlines both what the student can do by themselves and what they can do with the help of a more experienced person. Vygotsky believed that:

- What a student can do today with assistance, the student will in time be able to do by themselves.
- What a student can do with assistance is always more than what they can do by themselves.

This approach stresses the role of the more experienced person and the language of communication. Vygotsky coined the term **scaffolding**. Scaffolding is a process where through talking, a more skilled individual is trying to impart their knowledge to a less skilled individual. Effective communication involves the student and teacher coming to a shared understanding. In the previous case study (1.1), recall that Sam did not know the difference between a square and a rectangle. In this example the teaching assistant needed to explain to Sam the difference between a rectangle and square in such a way that (and this is the hard part) Sam's understanding of a rectangle and square would become the same as her understanding.

Vygotsky and Piaget had different views in regard to maturational readiness, that is, at what age, or stage of development, a child would be ready to learn new knowledge. For example, if a student had difficulty understanding a concept, i.e. the difference between a square and a rectangle, Piaget would say that:

- The student would need to discover the concept for themselves, in this case, by exploring different shapes.
- If the student could not grasp or understand the concept then their mind was just not ready to understand but in time, when their

mind had developed sufficiently, then they would be able to understand.

Vygotsky, however, believed that thinking and understanding was developed through communication and dialogue and therefore rather than wait for the thinking processes to mature, thinking and understanding could be brought on by the effective use of scaffolding. (See Chapter 2 for a more in-depth discussion of scaffolding.)

The behaviourist view

Behaviourists believe that individuals' behaviour is controlled or determined by what happens to them in the environment. Behaviour can be explained by the principles of reinforcement and punishment. Simply put behaviourists believe that:

- If behaviour is rewarded then the behaviour will increase. A reward will always result in an increase in the behaviour.
- If behaviour is punished then the behaviour will decrease. A punishment will always result in a decrease in the behaviour.

This theory is deceptively simple as what is considered a punishment and what is considered a reward depends very much on the individual. Consider the following:

Case study 1.2

James is in a Year 10 maths class. James hates maths and he hates his teacher, who he feels is always having a go at him. Today James has brought a beetle into class. When the teacher discovers the beetle on James's desk, the teacher insists that James remove the beetle at once. James says that the beetle is his best friend and that he will not stay in class if his best friend can't. The other students find this very amusing. The teacher needless to say is not amused and sends James out. The teacher thought he was punishing James, but James was thrilled, as he would do anything to get out of maths.

What this example shows is that being sent out of class was perceived not as punishment (as believed by the teacher) but as a reward. The teacher without realising it was actually reinforcing, or rewarding, playing up behaviour.

Another approach to learning explains how individuals learn what is called **conditioned emotional responses**. This term refers to a type of learning that results in certain events and situations being associated with particular emotions and feelings. When a person states that they have a fear of reading out loud that can be traced back to some nasty experience that occurred when they were young, they are, without realising it, talking about conditioned emotional responses. Now conditioned emotional responses can be explained by **classical conditioning** and this is where it gets complicated. Classical conditioning involves associating the automatic reactions caused by one event to other events that just happened to be occurring at the same time. To understand this terminology let's look at the following case study detailing how one man learned to fear reading out loud.

Case study 1.3

Rodney is a fifty-five-year-old successful businessman. Rodney reminisces regarding his experiences at school. 'My school was very strict. I remember this one day in English. Mr Teddington singled me out and told me to stand up and read a passage from Dickens's book *Great Expectations*. Well, I didn't like reading out loud and I stumbled over my words. Mr Teddington glared at me and bellowed: "You silly boy, read it again." So I did, but I still made mistakes. He just said: "You are going to read it until you get it right." Well, I spent the next twenty minutes reading that passage. At the end I was shaking, sweating and on the verge of bursting into tears. Well, after that I was never any good at English. I hated going to English classes and to this day I still can't read out loud in front of groups.'

This is quite an extreme example. However, Rodney's learned hatred of English classes and his learned fear of reading out loud in front of groups can be traced back to what happened in Mr Teddington's class and this can be analysed in classical conditioning terms.

Unconditioned stimulus	elicits/	**Unconditioned response**
A stimulus which has the natural ability to evoke a reflex response	leads to	*A reflex response elicited by the unconditioned stimulus*
(In this case the unconditioned stimulus is being insulted by the teacher		In this case the unconditioned response is to feel humiliated and upset)

Conditioned stimulus	elicits/	**Conditioned response**
A stimulus which comes to elicit a response by being associated with an unconditioned stimulus	leads to	*A response elicited by a conditioned stimulus*
(In this case the conditioned stimulus is being in an English class and reading out loud to a group of people)		(In this case the conditioned response is to associate fear and humiliation with being in an English class and reading out loud to a group of people)

What this example illustrates is that for learning to be successful, learning must *not* be associated with negative emotional experiences as these negative experiences could be associated with the learning environment.

The social learning approach

The social learning approach states that we learn by observing and imitating others. Simply put observational learning can be described by the command to watch and learn. This view states that an individual can start to behave in a certain way without previously being rewarded for that behaviour. In this case a person has watched how another person behaves and has observed what has happened to them in terms of being rewarded or punished. This relates to the ability which Piaget termed deferred imitation (see p. 12). When psychologists talk about the dangers of children watching violent films, what they fear is that children will watch the aggression in films and then at some later point imitate this aggressive behaviour in real life. However, observational learning is an important part of the learning process as children can imitate both desirable and undesirable behaviour.

Albert Bandura, an influential North American psychologist (1977) felt that there were four component parts to observational learning, these being:

• *Attentional processes.* We cannot imitate others unless we first pay attention to what others are doing.

- *Retentional processes.* As we may not imitate the behaviour for some time we need a way of remembering, that is, storing and organising in our mind what we have seen.
- *Motor reproduction processes.* This involves both remembering what to do and the necessity to practise the behaviour. For example we might want to learn to ice skate. We might have watched skaters like Torville and Dean many times. However, the first time we put on skates and venture on to the ice we will not be able to imitate what they do.
- *Motivational processes.* Though we have acquired knowledge of a behaviour we do not necessarily imitate the behaviour. In other words, we see people do many things that we would not dream of imitating. So what leads to imitation? The motivation to imitate depends on whether we think we can perform the behaviour and what we think will happen to us if we do.

The person we imitate is called a model. The model might be an actual person (an admired classmate) or the model might be symbolic, for example a cartoon character (Bart Simpson) or a film character (Luke Skywalker). **Social learning theory** states that children are more likely to imitate:

- Models who are similar to themselves, i.e. the same sex.
- Models who have been rewarded for their behaviour.
- Models who have power or status (strength, fame, special abilities).

Language and communication skills

The ability to communicate is essential to what it is to be human. But how do we communicate? Most of us communicate with a recognised language, be it English, French or Urdu. But even if we did not have language we could still communicate through facial expressions and body language. Indeed many of us can tell stories of how we were on holiday in some location where we did not know the language but still we somehow managed to make ourselves understood. Then there are those individuals who are deaf and who perhaps use an alternative system such as British Sign Language. There are some individuals who due to a combination of disabilities might use systems such as communication boards or Makaton. (For further discussion see Chapter 4.)

The point that is being made here is that there are many different ways of communicating and that spoken language is only one form of communication. All languages share certain common features. All languages use symbols. These symbols can be words, or they can be signs. The symbols themselves are arbitrary. For example the word *dog* looks and sounds nothing like what it represents and indeed different languages have different words that mean dog. What is important is that all speakers of the language understand these shared meanings. The next feature is that language is governed by rules such as word order. For example we know that 'Timmy kisses Mummy' is not the same as 'Mummy kisses Timmy'. Finally there is a creative element to language which we can see in poetry and in the way that language changes and evolves over time.

The extent of an individual's language can be expressed in terms of receptive and expressive abilities. **Receptive language** describes how much an individual can understand, while **expressive language** outlines how much an individual can communicate. In the course of normal development, a child learning to speak will always understand more than they can say.

Stages of language acquisition

Early language development

Babies are born with the ability to discriminate, that is, hear the difference, between all possible human speech sounds. This ability disappears well before the end of the first year, at which time the child will only be able to recognise those speech sounds which occur in its native language. From very early on conversation skills are developed and practised. Psychologists have observed how mothers will talk to their young babies. In such conversations a mother will treat the baby as an equal participant (Snow 1977). Imagine the following:

MOTHER: You are a lovely baby. (Pauses.)
BABY: (Moving its arms while looking at mother.)
MOTHER: Is that right?

It is through such dialogues that conversation skills such as turn-taking begin to develop.

From about one month on the baby starts cooing (making vowel sounds). At five months the baby begins babbling (repeating one syllable over and over again). About this time and well before the baby utters its first words the baby will use its eyes to communicate with people. A baby will follow their mother's eyes, catch her attention and then move their eyes to something which they want their mother to see. The ability to follow another person's gaze is called **gaze monitoring** and is essential to language development. For example a mother might look at the bus and say: 'There's our bus.' Now if the baby is to eventually associate a bus with the word *bus* then it is crucial that the baby follows their mother's gaze and looks at what their mother is looking at. If a child did not have this ability to follow another's gaze then language development would be effected. If mom said 'look at the bus' and the child was looking at a lamp-post then the child might think that the word 'bus' was associated with the object *lamp-post*. This could lead to the child calling lamp-posts buses.

Babies will also use pointing. **Instrumental pointing** involves pointing at something that they want , but that they can't get for themselves, e.g. the biscuit jar on the top shelf. **Proto-declarative pointing**, on the other hand, is pointing with the intention of sharing an experience, e.g. baby points to lady in a large hat as if to say: 'Just look at that hat!' At eleven to twelve months babbling becomes more speech-like in form and has the same intonation and emphasis as adult speech. It is at this point that babies from different nationalities will sound different. The first words will appear around about twelve months.

Development of grammar

At about eighteen months the child is using one-word sentences, which have been defined as **holophrases**. Holophrases involve the use of one word in combination with gestures. For example a child points at a chocolate biscuit, jumps up and down while still pointing and says: 'biscuit'. The next stage has been described as **telegraphic speech.** At this stage the child will use only the key essential words. For example if you ask a child from about twenty to twenty-four months to say 'I am eating a chocolate biscuit,' they will probably say, 'Eat biscuit.' As the child begins to use more words to create longer sentences, the child begins to experiment with and understand the rules which determine how words should be put together to form meaningful sentences. One common occurrence is **over-regularisation** or **over-generalisation** of rules. For example, at some time around about three years of age the child will learn that past tense is indicated by putting the sound *ed* at the end of a verb, e.g. 'Dogs growl. Yesterday the dog growled at me.' However, English is a complicated language and there are many exceptions. Children between the ages of three and five will often make mistakes regarding the over-generalisation of rules and say such things as 'I goed shopping for biscuits.'

Theories of language learning

It is important to note that children learn language in a social context.
Bruner (1983) talked of formats that are of **repetitive routines**, which allow children to break the code of language. Repetitive routines refer to daily events in a child's life such as getting ready to go out, meal times and having a bath. Let's look at the following:

Case study 1.4

BABY (pointing at the biscuit jar while jumping up and down): Biq! Biq! Biq!
MOTHER: Does my little boy want a biscuit? Here you go. Here is a nice biscuit, a nice biscuit. (Mom hands over the biscuit.)

Some months later

TODDLER (pointing at the biscuit jar while jumping up and down): Me biscuit!
MOTHER: You want a biscuit. What do we say? 'May I have a biscuit, please?'
TODDLER: Biscuit now! Biscuit now!
MOTHER: What do we say? 'May I have a biscuit, please?'
TODDLER: Biscuit please.
MOTHER: That's a good boy. Here's the biscuit.

Some time later

CHILD: Mom! Give me a biscuit!
MOTHER: Say it properly. 'May I have a biscuit, please?'
CHILD: May I have a biscuit, please?
MOTHER: That's a good boy. Now here's two of your favourite chocolate chip biscuits. Now what do you say?

The above example illustrates many points, one being that language develops within a social context. It is clear that the 'asking for a biscuit' activity was what Bruner (1983) referred to as a repetitive routine or format. It is interesting to note that the mother's language over time remained very much the same. Bruner would say that it is due to parents saying the same things in the same way in reference to the same activity, day in, day out, that children can begin to break the code of language. Other psychologists (Snow and Ferguson 1977; Schachter and Strage 1982) have talked about the style of language that is used with very young children. The term they use is **motherese**:

- Speakers of motherese will usually speak in a higher-pitch voice and at a slower pace.
- Sentences are shorter and usually grammatically correct.
- Sentences are grammatically simple.
- Repetition is used often.
- Vocabulary is concrete in that it refers to objects or people that are present.

Learning theory of language development

What differed in the above example was what the mother expected of the child and what was consequently rewarded. The above example illustrates the learning theory of language development, in that language is learned through imitation and reinforcement. At the start of the example the child can only say 'biq', but saying 'biq' is rewarded by receiving the chocolate biscuit. To begin with the mother is re-inforcing appropriate sounds but over time what she is reinforcing changes from sounds to meaningful words to grammatically correct sentences. Though the principles of learning can explain some aspects of language development they cannot adequately explain the creative nature of language. The learning approach cannot explain how children will sometimes say things that they have never heard.

Nativist theory of language development

Another approach to language, which can explain the creative nature of language, states that rather than being learned, language ability is pre-programmed into the mind and that language ability emerges slowly as the individual matures. Chomsky (1965) outlined what he referred to as a **language acquisition device**: that something within our brain that we are born with which allows us to develop language. Children from this viewpoint are seen as grammar machines. This approach sees the language environment as important as it triggers the development of the language acquisition device. One assumption of this approach is that it is easier to learn a language before puberty than afterwards and that the earlier an individual learns a language the easier it is. This view is termed the **critical period hypothesis**.

An interactional theory of language development

Nowadays many theorists state that the learning theory and the nativist theory of language development, outlined here, are both correct. In a sense, language development can best be explained by an interaction between a maturing individual and their learning experiences.

Bilingual acquisition

An interesting area of current research concerning language is the acquisition of two languages. **Bilingual acquisition** can be **simultaneous**, that is, the child, from infancy, will learn two languages at the same time. An example of this would be where the father is French and the mother is English and that the parents wish the child to learn both languages. Usually, where this is the case, parents teach the child two languages by using the one person–one language rule, that is, Dad will speak French to the child, while Mom speaks English. The second form of bilingualism is called **sequential** and this involves the child first learning one language and then at some later stage being introduced to a second language. An example of this would be an Italian child who is fluent only in Italian, moving to England at the age of five and having at that point to learn English.

Stages in simultaneous language acquisition (Watson 1995)

1   Words from both languages are learned by associating words with concepts. For example a child may point to a dog and say 'dog–chien', that is, both the English and French words for dog. Sometimes these two words may be blended or combined in some form.
2   The child is learning to speak in both languages and increasingly realises that there are two separate systems of communication, but will make mistakes in terms of grammatical structure. For example they might attempt to combine the two or apply the

right grammatical rules to the wrong language. This phase may last for one to two years.

3   The child is now fluent in two languages. The child may have learned to rigidly associate one language with one person or context. For example, they only speak Italian on weekends when Grandma comes to stay.

Processes and stages in sequential language acquisition (Watson 1995)

This theory assumes that the child is fluent in its first language and uses the first language as a starting point from which to learn the second. It is helpful at this stage to think of our example of a five-year-old Italian boy who moves to England.

- *Interactional phase.* As social relationships are central to children, children will first learn key phrases that help them to interact and play with other children. These key phrases would include 'Can I play?', 'My turn' and 'No.'
- *Interference.* Here the child is using the rules of its first language and trying to apply them to the second language. This will result in errors.
- *Silent period.* Some children will speak very little when they are first exposed to the second language. This phase can possibly last several months. It is thought that this phase allows the child to build up an understanding of what is being said around them. However, not all children go through this stage and the extent of this stage is thought to be determined by the child's learning style and personality.
- *Code switching.* This is where the child switches from one language to the other in mid-stream, so to speak. This is quite normal and often children do this as they are imitating adults within their culture who are bilingual.
- *Language loss.* This is where one language has replaced the other. In an extreme example the child will be exposed to the new language but have no one to talk to in their first language and thus while learning the second language they will probably lose some of their abilities in their first.

According to the critical period hypothesis, a child before puberty will find it easier to learn a second language than an adult as their brain is more flexible. It is thought that children who learn a second language will take from one to two years to achieve **basic interpersonal communication skills** (language first learned by toddlers and pre-schoolers) and five to seven years to acquire **cognitive academic language proficiency** (the language used within classroom contexts and the standard necessary to cope with GCSEs) (Cummins 1984).

Social and emotional skills

Psychologists have described people as social animals. Social inter-action, being involved with others, is a vital element of most people's lives. Though we may be able to remember how we learned to read and write most of us will find it difficult to say how we learned to interact with others. Social and emotional skills are not specifically taught in school, but somewhere along the line most of us will have learned enough skills to get by. Most of us will be able to think of people who are very good at social skills. These individuals appear confident and relaxed in social gatherings and seem to be very good at knowing just the right thing to say. On the other hand we probably know people who stand too close to others in lifts, who are extremely awkward and never say the right thing.

Theory of mind

Psychologists now believe that in order to fully engage in the social world we need to develop a theory of mind. A **theory of mind** involves the awareness that:

- As you have thoughts, emotions and feelings, so do other people.
- As your beliefs about the world influence your behaviour, other people's behaviour will be influenced by their beliefs.
- Different people will have different beliefs.
- By watching what a person does you can to some extent guess what they are thinking and feeling.

Researchers (Baron-Cohen *et al.* 1985) investigated the concept of theory of mind by giving children what has become known as the Sally–Ann task. The task goes like this:

- Sally and Ann are both in the room.
- While Ann is watching Sally hides the marble under the basket.
- Sally leaves the room.

- Ann takes the marble from the basket and hides the marble under the box.
- Ann leaves.
- Sally returns.

The child is then asked: 'Where will Sally look for her marble?' We know that the marble is now hidden under the box because we saw Ann hide it there. But we also know that Sally *doesn't know what we know* as she did not see Ann take the marble from its original hiding place and hide it somewhere else. Therefore Sally is going to look for the marble in the place where she hid it. This kind of reasoning involves a theory of mind and this skill is developed by most children by the age of four.

The development of empathy

Empathy is an important social skill. Hoffman (1982) saw empathy as first matching or experiencing the same emotion as another person and that this heightened emotion would lead to an increased desire to help. Hoffman saw empathy developing in stages. The stages are:

1 *Global empathy.* This develops during the first year. At this stage the young child will match the emotions of the other person. For example, if a young child sees his mother crying he will cry too.
2 *Egocentric empathy.* This stage begins to develop from about twelve to eighteen months. Again the child responds to the other's distress with distress of their own, but then goes on to offer comfort. However, what they offer as comfort tends to be what they themselves would find comforting. A young child who observes mother crying as she has just caught her finger in the door might offer mom their favourite teddy.
3 *Empathy for another's feelings.* This stage begins at about two to three years of age. Here the child both recognises and partially matches the emotion. For example, a four-year-old child will realise that their eighteen-month-old brother is upset and be upset themselves but not to the same degree. Again the child will offer something as a comfort, but now will offer an appropriate item of comfort. In this case, the four-year-old will not give her eighteen-month-old brother her own favourite teddy, but will quickly search for her brother's blanket that he likes to chew. As children grow older they become more able at recognising a wider range of emotions.

4 *Empathy for another's life condition.* This stage begins in late child-
   hood or adolescence, corresponding to Piaget's stage of formal
   operations. The child now has developed a more generalised
   view of others' feelings and can imagine how individuals might
   feel in certain situations. For example, what it is like for children
   growing up in countries that are afflicted with famine.

Though Hoffman has outlined stages in regards to empathy, perhaps
the more interesting question relates to how children learn to express
concern for others. Children learn how to be thoughtful and considerate by observing others being thoughtful and considerate. This
is a clear example of observational learning. It is helpful to tell children
to be thoughtful and considerate, but it is essential to do what you say.
If there is a conflict between what you say and what you do, children
will imitate what you do. This is an example of actions speaking louder
than words.

Stages in friendship

Selman and Jaquette (1977) outlined stages in the understanding of
friendship. You will notice that the age at which a child enters a
stage will vary.

- Age 3–7   *Momentary playmates.* A friend is someone who you
  play with.
- Age 4–9   *One-way assistance.* A friend is someone who helps you.
  However, the idea that you help your friend has not
  been fully developed.
- Age 6–12 *Fair weather co-operation.* A friendship involves helping
  each other out. However, friendships at this stage can
  be fragile as minor setbacks or conflicts can result in
  the breaking of the friendship.
- Age 9–15 *Intimate friendship.* Involves intimacy, mutuality and
  will continue despite minor setbacks and conflicts.
- Age 12+   *Autonomous interdependence.* Friendships involve intimacy and mutuality but friendships grow and change
  with time. A friend is not possessive but recognises
  and accepts their own and their friend's need for
  other relationships.

Much research has focused on the importance of friendships. Mannarino (1980) compared pre-adolescents who had stable friends with those who didn't and found that those who had stable friendships had higher measures of altruism and self-concept, that is, the children were seen as more helpful and appeared more confident and happy within themselves. Cowen *et al.* (1973) found that adults who had been referred to mental health professionals were two and a half times more likely to have had difficulties with making friends at eight years of age. In a large-scale review of studies in this area Parker and Asher (1987) found a consistent link between low peer acceptance and an increased likelihood of dropping out of school and a consistent link between aggressiveness to peers and later involvement in juvenile and adult crime. It is important to realise that these studies are highlighting links and that they are *not* saying that difficulties in friendship *cause* later problems in life. Obviously there are many reasons why teenagers get involved in juvenile crime and why adults are referred to mental health services. However, as it seems that friendships are important other researchers have focused on trying to help children who have difficulties making friends. Furman *et al.* (1979) identified four- and five-year-old children who seldom played with other children. They arranged for these children to have special play sessions with younger children. It was hoped that through playing with younger children, play activities could be practised and that this would lead them to feel more confident in social interactions. This did seem to help. O'Connor (1972) worked with a group of junior school children that had been identified as shy and withdrawn. These children were shown a film of a shy withdrawn student who gradually and slowly over time became increasingly better at relating to other children. It was hoped that the children would imitate what they had seen on the film and again this proved successful. Oden and Asher (1977) specifically taught socially isolated eight- and nine-year-olds specific skills such as how to co-operate, communicate and participate with other children. These children were seen to improve on social interactions and these improvements could still be seen a year later.

Emotional intelligence

More recently psychologists have been interested in the topic of **emotional intelligence**. Emotional intelligence is more than being socially skilled, being a nice person or behaving well. For Goleman (1996) an emotionally intelligent person is a person who:

• Knows and manages their own feelings well.
• Reads and deals effectively with other people's feelings.
• Can motivate themselves and persist in the face of frustrations.
• Can control impulse and delay gratification.
• Can regulate their moods and keep distress from swamping the ability to think.
• Can empathise and hope. (Pickard 1999, pp. 55-6.)

Goleman (1996) sees the goal as: 'raising the level of social and emotional competence in children as part of their regular education – not just something taught remedially to children who are faltering and identified as "troubled," but a set of skills and understandings essential for every child' (p. 262). Such programmes include components on self-awareness, personal decision making, managing feelings, handling stress, developing empathy, becoming a good communicator, self-disclosure, insight, self-acceptance, personal responsibility, assertiveness, group dynamics and conflict resolution. One example, which involves teaching impulse control to Year 5 students, involved a stop-light poster with six steps. Students were encouraged to go through these steps if they felt very angry and wanted to hit someone, or if they felt very upset and wanted to burst into tears. The steps were:

Red light	1	Stop, calm down, and think before you act
Yellow light	2	Say the problem and how you feel
	3	Set a positive goal
	4	Think of lots of solutions
	5	Think ahead to the consequences
Green Light	6	Go ahead and try the best plan

(Goleman 1996, p. 276)

Specific skills

Development of reading

Though we may not be able to remember how we learned to talk, most people will have vivid memories of learning to read and write. We may remember with some fondness our earliest readers, be they about 'Biff and Chip' or 'Janet and John'. We may remember how we learned to hold a pencil and how we felt when we had mastered joined-up writing. Much of the early school years focuses on literacy, which encompasses both reading and writing skills. Reading has been defined as the ability to extract meaning from the text. The skill of writing, while being related to reading, involves the fine motor skills involved in putting pen to paper and the ability to spell. In English, spelling is perceived by many as more difficult than reading and on average there is about a year's gap between learning to read new words and learning to spell these words.

Reading is said to involve both **top-down** and **bottom-up** processing. Top-down processing refers to our knowledge of the world, including our knowledge of our spoken language and how we use this knowledge to guide us in our understanding of the text. Imagine that a young child of five is asked to read the following: 'The duck said quack.' Now the child recognises the words: *the*, *duck* and *said*, but the child does not recognise the last word. The child has never seen the word *quack* written. However, from the child's understanding of the world and her knowledge of language, she knows that ducks say 'quack', so the child is able from the context to guess the last word. Here the child is using top-down processing to help her read the text.

Bottom-up processing on the other hand states that we create meaning by recognising first the letters that make up the words, then the sound combinations that these letters make and then finally we put these sound combinations together as words. Imagine a child of seven is asked to read the following:'The witch raised her wand and said: "Olly-olly-tri-ma-golly".' If the child is to successfully read the witch's spell, then they will need to know the rules which state that certain letter combinations correspond to certain sounds. This example illustrates both bottom-up processing and **grapheme–phoneme awareness**.

Often children who have difficulty in learning to read are said to have a poor grapheme–phoneme awareness. **Graphemes** can be defined as the letters of the alphabet. The letters of the alphabet alone, or in combination, correspond to particular **phonemes** or sound units. For example the word *cat* is made up of three phonemes, *kuh-aah-tuh*, and these sound units/phonemes correspond to the letters/graphemes of *c a t*. Therefore children who have difficulty in recognising the link between letters and sounds will find reading and spelling difficult.

The English language is a difficult language to learn to read and spell for a number of reasons. To begin with, a child learning to read will have to come to grips with the twenty-six letters of the alphabet and the forty-four sound combinations that these letters can make. Further, Bailey (1967) states that there are about 200 rules for combining sounds. One rule, the two-vowel rule, states that the first vowel says its name while the second is silent. However, there are always exceptions to the rules. So while the rule holds true for words such as *tie* and *eat* it does not work for a word such as *field*.

Frith (1985) sees reading developing through the following three stages:

- *Logographic*, age 3–5. In this phase the child responds to text on a sight recognition basis. A young child of three might recognise the signs for Tesco or McDonald's. Here the child is not reading the individual letters but is responding to the particular visual pattern that the word makes. The look and say method utilises this strategy for reading. However, this approach has its limitations as children will often make mistakes between visually similar words such as *black* and *block*.
- *Alphabetic*, age 5–7. This stage involves the child developing a phonological awareness, that is, an awareness that certain letters correspond to certain sounds. With a knowledge of phonics, a beginning reader can start to sound out unfamiliar words.
- *Orthographic*, age 7–9+. This stage involves the child recognising words by sight as distinctive letter combinations. The child does not have to sound out the word; the child recognises the unique letter combinations that identify the word.

Concentration, attention and memory

It is generally believed that a child's ability to concentrate, pay attention and remember is poorer than that of an adult and that these abilities develop with time. Certainly young children have difficulties remembering their telephone number and address. Young children are limited in the time that they can actually sit and listen to the teacher. However, in saying that, young children can memorise and retell their favourite story and even the most fidgety student can often sit and play a video game for hours. It seems that memory for some events is easier than others. When an event is personally interesting or meaningful we are not aware that we are remembering; memory just happens. However, when we are asked to remember an item which is not personally meaningful, the act of remembering needs to be conscious and deliberate.

The skills of concentration, attention and memory are interrelated. For example let us imagine a Year 2 student who is trying to learn a list of spelling words for a test on Friday. To learn the words:

• The child must pay *attention*, that is, the child must focus on those specific words.
• Then the child must *concentrate*, that is, the child must focus on those words, specifically the individual letters that make up those words.
• Finally the child must *remember* this information, that is, the child must commit the information to memory.

When we talk about the processes involved in remembering we are talking about memory. Memory involves three stages. The stages are **encoding, storage** and **retrieval**. First the individuals must encode the information to be learned. Information can be encoded either verbatim, that is word for word, or the gist of the event can be stored. How the information is to be encoded depends on the task. If a list of spelling words is to be remembered then the memory has to be letter for letter. However, if you were asked to remember what happened in a film, then you would not remember the film word for word, rather you would remember the gist of the film, that is, the essence or key points. Once information is encoded it is stored. According to Piaget information will be stored in the form of schemas (see p. 10). Once information is stored then it can be retrieved later or recollected when needed.

Memory has also been thought of as being divided into short-term or working memory and long-term memory. Short-term/working memory consists of everything we are currently thinking about at any one point in time. Long-term memory is where we store information. Information in long-term memory is transferred into our short-term/working memory when the need arises.

It has been found that the capacity of short-term memory, that is, the amount of information that we can hold in our short-term memory, increases over the years until as adults we can hold seven (plus or minus two) units of information. Asking a person to immediately recall a string of random digits (e.g. 8 4 5 2 9 6 1 3) tests this capacity. Research has revealed that as children become older they realise that in order to remember unrelated information (how to spell dinosaur, their times tables) they must do something special with this information. This something special is referred to as a **memory strategy**. Ornstein *et al.* (1975) compared strategies used by Year 3 and Year 8 students when asked to remember a list of words which the teacher read out loud to them. The teacher would read a list of words (such as cow, table, cup, tree and car). The students were asked to repeat the words out loud as they heard them. This is what the younger students did. However, the older students while saying the new word would also take the time to rehearse the previous words. Miller (1990) noted differences in approaches to homework. Year 8 students were better at selecting relevant material and ignoring irrelevant material than younger students. It also seems that to remember unrelated information, it is important not only that the information is stored but also that the information is organised and that organisation improves recall.

It would be nice to think that all information taught at school was personally meaningful and that memory would just happen. Part of the reason behind a child being actively involved in the learning process is to create learning situations that are meaningful. However, the reality is that most students at some point will struggle to remember what is taught. Recent research has focused on **metamemory**, that is, the knowledge someone has of their own memory processes. In terms of encouraging children to remember what is being taught in school, children need to realise that they need to put an effort into remembering, and that remembering unrelated information requires memory strategies. Children need to be aware of what strategy they are using and to monitor whether the strategy is working or not. Further if the strategy is not working then the children need to be able to find another strategy.

Mathematical skills

Much time is spent on teaching children maths. But first it is helpful to define what we mean by maths. Bell *et al.* (1983) believed that teaching maths involved the learning of facts, skills, concepts, strategies, attitudes and finally an appreciation of maths. The above were defined as:

- *Facts.*
  Abbreviations, e.g. cm for centimetres.
  Conventions, e.g. $6x$ means six times x.
  Conversion factors, e.g. $32°$ Fahrenheit $= 0°$ Celsius.
  Concepts, e.g. even numbers.
  Factual results, e.g. results of times tables.
- *Skills.* Skills are defined as a set of multi-step procedures that can be used in certain specific situations. For example, if a student is given the question $\frac{1}{2} + \frac{1}{4}$, a student who is competent in maths would realise that the first step in solving the problem is to find a common denominator for the fractions: $\frac{1}{2} + \frac{1}{4} = \frac{2}{4} + \frac{1}{4} = \frac{3}{4}$.
- *Concepts.* A concept refers to a property of an object. For example, all negative numbers are numbers less than zero.
- *General strategies.* A general strategy refers to ways of approaching a problem. A general strategy can be applied to many different types of problem. For example, when a student is asked to add $16 + 14$ in their head, the student could come up with a strategy of simplifying the problem ($16 + 14 = 10 + 10 + 6 + 4 = 30$). Simplification in this case is a general strategy.
- *Attitudes.* Attitudes refers to a person's feelings and emotional responses. It is hoped that students come to enjoy and feel confident about maths.
- *Appreciation.* An appreciation of maths involves the student realising the usefulness of maths in society and everyday life.

It is the aim of the National Curriculum to specifically teach strategies that relate to using, communicating and developing ideas of argument or proof in mathematics. Mathematical skills, like many skills, build on previously learned knowledge. It is hoped that the way in which maths is taught will develop a positive attitude and appreciation of maths. What is first taught in schools lays the foundation for what is taught later. A student must master the initial concepts before they can move on and understand later concepts. For example, if a child does not understand what is meant by 'more than' or 'less than', the child cannot answer the question whether 17 is more than 15. Piaget's views on learning as an interaction between the child being actively involved with his environment and maturation are central to maths teaching. Maturation limits what can be taught at certain ages. Piaget's views on the development of logic have influenced when mathematical concepts are introduced. For example could you teach a child of four their times tables? Possibly a four-year-old could memorise 'four times four is sixteen' but would they really understand what is meant by multiplication? Real learning involves more than receiving and repeating back the knowledge parrot-fashion. Real learning involves making sense of the knowledge. Psychologists have described this process as constructing knowledge. Vygotsky's views on how knowledge is learned through social interaction is also central to mathematical teaching, in that children learn about maths by talking about how to do maths problems, that is, what strategies to use with a more experienced person.

The development of fine and gross motor skills

Learning to physically move (e.g. crawl, walk, skip, hold a pencil, juggle) involves both **biological maturation** and **interaction in the environment**. For example at a certain age we might develop the co-ordination to learn to skip but practice at skipping makes us better. To see an example of this one only has to watch Year 2 boys and girls competing in a skipping race. Learning a physical skill involves both learning the sequence of actions that make up a skill and how to combine the sequence such that the movement appears graceful. Physical movements can involve the whole body, e.g. jumping (**gross motor skills**) or more refined movements using only certain body parts, e.g. handwriting (**fine motor skills**). To organise physical movement an individual is dependent upon the body receiving sensory information from the environment. Sensory information is received by **tactile receptors**, the **vestibular apparatus** and **proprioceptive system** (Ripley *et al.* 1997). These are defined as follows:

- *Tactile receptors* are specialised cells within the skin that send information about light, touch, pain, temperature and pressure to the brain.
- *Vestibular receptors* are located within the inner ear and automatically co-ordinate movements of the eyes, head and body in order to maintain balance.
- *Proprioceptors* are present in the muscles and joints and enable an individual to move their arms and legs without visual guidance. For example we can do up the buttons on our coat without looking.

Any difficulties with processing sensory information could lead to problems with movement.

In looking at this area psychologists have developed a series of developmental milestones indicating what most children should be able to do at a certain age. Again it is important to stress that there will be individual differences. However, when a child is considerably delayed in reaching their developmental milestones this could indicate conditions such as dyspraxia. (See Chapter 4.) Some examples of developmental motor milestones would be:

- *Five months.* Can transfer one object from hand to hand.
- *One year.* Child pulls itself up to stand, walks around furniture.
- *Eighteen months.* Child begins to show a preference for one hand. Can throw and kick a ball without falling over.
- *Two and a half years.* Can remove or unfasten coat. Can put on simple items such as vest and pants.
- *Three and a half years.* Can walk on tiptoe. Can button up clothing. Can draw a person that includes head, eyes, nose, mouth and legs.
- *Six years.* Can hop and skip.

(Ripley *et al.* (1997). A full description of motor milestones can be found in Ripley *et al.* (1997), pp. 29–33, 41–2.)

Stages in handwriting (Ripley et al. 1997)

Early phase

- Establishing a support hand and a dominant hand. The dominant hand needs to practise the specialised movements that correspond to letters. The support hand needs to learn to move and hold the paper in position.
- Mastering the thumb and two-finger grip for holding pencils or pens.
- As skilled writing involves fine finger and wrist movements, the child will need to learn the basic movement patterns corresponding to letters and numbers.
- A child needs to master pencil control and maintain appropriate pressure on the paper.

Middle phase

- Involves learning to maintain an even letter size and to place the letters on a line.
- Being able to use a variety of writing tools.

Final phase

- Involves the speeding up of writing. Dutton (1989) reports that at the age of five a child can write up to one and a half words per minute and this progresses to an average of eighteen words per minute at the age of sixteen.

In England it is customary that children beginning school first learn to print. At the age of seven joined-up writing, or what is referred to as a cursive script, is introduced.

Reflective component

Case study 1.5

Sandra works in a reception class as a teaching assistant. Sandra described the following session in a workplace log.

Description of the event (What happened?)

It was Monday morning, just after break time, and I was to work with the Blue group on letters. It is always difficult when the children come in after play time. There were six children in the group. Eventually they all sat down. Harry started rocking on his chair. Emily dropped her pencil under the table and had to crawl under the table to get it. Robert and Sarah must have thought that crawling under the table was a fun game as they then dropped their pencils and now there were three children under the table. Mrs Smith saw what was happening and came over and said: 'That's enough. Children do not crawl under tables.' The children did not like to be told off by Mrs Smith and they quickly sat down in their seats. Eventually everyone was ready to work but it took at least five minutes to get started. The first activity was to play a game that involved learning the sequence of letters. I told the children that I would pick some letters from the middle of the alphabet and put them up in order on the magnetic board. We would then say all the letters together. After we had done this, I would turn the board round and take one of the letters away and then they would have to guess what letter was missing. The children really seemed to enjoy this. When they were trying to guess what letter was missing I made sure that everyone had a say before I told them what letter was missing. The children were very good at this task and I told them that they had all worked very hard and I gave them each a sticker.

Feelings (What did I feel? What do I think the students felt?)

On the whole I felt pleased. I think the children really enjoyed this session, though some of the children did not like it when Mrs Smith told them off. I wished I could have controlled the situation better so that it wasn't necessary for Mrs Smith to intervene.

Evaluation (What was good? What was difficult?)

The good thing about this session was that the children were actively involved in the game. The difficult bit was the beginning. I had difficulty getting the children under control.

Analysis (How do I make sense of what happened? Why did it happen?)

The best part of this was that the children were all actively involved. This relates to what Piaget termed **discovery learning**. The children learn about letter sequences by playing a game that involved this. The children also were encouraged by the praise I gave them and they were especially delighted by the stickers they received at the end. As I said the difficult bit was the beginning. It seemed here that observational learning was taking place. Robert and Sarah imitated what Emily was doing as it seemed like fun.

In conclusion (What could I have done?)

To begin with I should have set ground rules for behaving.

Action plan (What will I do next time?)

Next time I definitely will set ground rules.

Self-assessment

1 Is there anything else you would add to the workplace log?
2 What else could Sandra have done? (Remember to use the psychological principles that have been discussed in this chapter.)

Case study 1.6

Jane works as a teaching assistant in a large secondary school. Today she was in a Year 9 English class. In this class Jane was supporting Emily. When Jane arrived she noticed that Emily was crying. Jane quietly sat down beside Emily and asked what was the matter. Emily said that she had just had a fight with her best friend, Joanne. Joanne had tried to push her into the boys' toilet at break. Emily said real friends wouldn't do that. Emily picked up her book and threw it at Joanne. Joanne picked up her book and threw it back at Emily. This had all happened so quickly. Both girls were sent out and Jane took them to the behavioural unit for a chat. Jane reminded them about the school's rules on behaviour and how their behaviour was unacceptable. Both girls were quiet and sullen throughout. The bell went and the girls went to the next class. Needless to say, they would both be getting a detention for their behaviour. Jane felt that perhaps she should have said something different to the girls, but she wasn't sure what.

Self-assessment

Your task is to imagine that you are Jane and to complete a workplace log. Remember to use the headings (*Description of the event*, *Feelings*, *Evaluation*, *Analysis*, *In conclusion* and *Action plan*). Hint: try to apply some of the psychological concepts we have talked about in this chapter.

Chapter 2

Learning support strategies

Learning strategies as a way to promote effective learning

From our own experience as both a learner and as someone who works within a classroom we know that there are many different ways of teaching. A teacher will know and use a variety of methods to support learning. For example, how were you taught your times tables? Did you have to stand up with your class and recite your times tables? Were you taught your times tables as a class or did you work your way through math-cards? How are children today taught the times tables? The art of teaching or supporting learning is knowing a variety of methods and more importantly knowing when to use them. In this chapter when we talk about ways or methods of teaching we will be talking about learning support strategies. It is the aim of this chapter to outline a variety of learning support strategies.

To set the scene we are going to look at two case studies. These two case studies along with some case studies referred to in Chapter 1 will be used to explore a variety of learning support strategies. As a teaching assistant you will be working under the direction of the teacher. Many strategies which will be outlined in this chapter the teacher will actually design. However, as a teaching assistant, you might be asked to help the teacher carry out these strategies on a day-to-day basis. By understanding how and why the strategy works, hopefully you will be in a better position to support the teacher. Some of the strategies in this chapter you will be able to implement for yourself when you are supporting students individually or in groups.

Case study 2.1 An idea for learning about weight

Sarah, a teaching assistant, was working with a group of Year 1 children. Sarah had chosen five classroom objects and wrapped them in brightly coloured paper and covered them with bows. The children were very excited when they saw the packages. The children jumped up and down and kept asking whose birthday it was and when they could open the presents. Sarah explained to the children that they were going to play a game about weight. To play the game they had to decide which package was the heaviest. Sarah had each child in turn pick up the packages and give their ideas on which package was the heaviest and which was the lightest. The children took turns to weigh one parcel each. Each child would place the package on one side of the scale and use multi-link pieces to balance the scales. The children had to count and record how many multi-link pieces were needed to balance the scales.

Case study 2.2 Difficulty with essays

Donna, a teaching assistant, was working in a Year 9 English class. The teacher talked about adverts and how adverts are an example of persuasive speech. The students were given a handout that contained four adverts regarding the merits of Tenerife. The students were asked to write a short essay comparing the differences between two adverts in terms of form, purpose, audience, content, language and presentation. The teacher gave the students fifteen minutes at the end of class to start the essay and told the class to hand in the assignment the next week. Donna was working with a small group of students who found it difficult to write essays. Though the teacher had stressed that an essay contained an introduction, a middle bit with facts and an ending, which involved writing their own thoughts and conclusions, these students struggled and seemed not to know where to begin.

Discovery/active learning

Piaget would describe the lesson on weight as an example of discovery learning. Piaget believed that individuals had to be actively involved in the learning process. Imagine you were trying to teach a child about weight. You could, in order to teach the concept of weight, give the following definition: 'the degree of heaviness of a thing, especially as measured on a balance or weighing machine. Expressed according to units of measurement (e.g. kilos, tons, etc.). Apples are usually sold by weight.'

What would a child learn from such an example? Some children might be able to memorise such a definition, but would they really understand what weight meant? According to Piaget, to really understand a concept you have to be actively involved. Therefore as in the case study children learn about weight by holding and measuring different objects. Active involvement leads to the development of schemas, units of mental thought.

In discovery learning the teacher or teaching assistant needs to encourage the expansion of existing schemas and the development of new schemas. Sometimes, when teaching a child, it is very clear to the teacher or teaching assistant that the child has no idea or the completely wrong idea about a concept. For example in the previous chapter (Case study 1.1) we looked at the example of Sam, who believed that squares and rectangles were the same as they had four corners. At this point the teacher or teaching assistant must ask questions or create situations where the child realises for himself that there is a contradiction between what they believe to be true, their reality, and what everyone else believes to be true, a shared reality. A discovery learning activity focusing on the differences between squares and rectangles could involve students, such as Sam, measuring the sides of rectangles and squares and writing these down. By participating in such an activity Sam could learn for himself the difference between squares and rectangles. It is also possible that other children can provide contrasting views. When a child experiences contrasting or differing views to his/her own this is called socio-cognitive conflict.

In summary discovery learning involves:

- Assessing what the child knows and does not know.
- Asking questions or providing activities that create the need to expand existing schemas or creating new schemas.

The spiral curriculum

Bruner, an American psychologist, developed the concept of the **spiral curriculum**. The spiral curriculum involves teaching the same concepts at different ages but with increasing complexity. This can be seen within the National Curriculum, where topics are introduced in the earliest years and revisited in later years but in more detail. Bruner (1963) stated that any subject can be taught effectively and in some intellectually honest form to any child at any stage of development.

Linked to the idea of the spiral curriculum are Bruner's views on how thinking develops. Bruner outlined three ways or modes of thinking or processing information. These modes of thinking develop with time. These modes of representation are:

- *Enactive representation.* This form of memory can be likened to a muscle memory and begins at birth. Examples of this muscle memory would include a baby learning to grasp a rattle or a baby learning to crawl. This form of memory continues throughout adult life. Examples of this muscle memory in later life would be learning to drive.
- *Iconic mode.* This way of thinking develops from the age of one. Information is encoded or remembered in the form of mental images or pictures. Information is also remembered as smells or sounds.
- *The symbolic mode.* This way of processing information develops around the age of seven. This way of remembering involves using symbols and codes. Examples of symbols and codes are language and mathematical rules. For example we often learn how to do a task by remembering in words what to do, e.g. when logging on to the internet we will remind ourselves that we need to click on a certain icon and we need to key in a password.

According to Bruner the way in which a subject is taught to a young child should correspond to a child's mode of representation or their current way of thinking. Bruner would say that children over seven and adults could use all ways of thinking or modes of representation. Table 2.1 illustrates how the concept of weight could be taught at various ages.

Scaffolding

Vygotsky introduced the concept of scaffolding. However, in more recent years it has been psychologists such as Bruner that have developed and expanded on this idea.

As a learning support strategy scaffolding relates to effective instruction. For Vygotsky the language of instruction is everything. Instruction needs to correspond to the student's ability, that is, when the student is struggling more help is given and when the student is

Table 2.1 The spiral curriculum

Stage	Example of teaching style
Enactive. Memory is encoded in the muscles whenever the individual physically acts on its environment. This type of memory develops from birth	A very young child could learn about weight by lifting objects. A small teddy is easier to carry around than the 3 ft teddy Daddy won at the fair
Iconic. A child between the ages of one and seven uses mental images based on sight, touch, hearing and smell	A class of Year 1 children take turns weighing parcels of different sizes on a scale. The students use multi-link pieces to balance the scales
Symbolic. Individuals of seven and above are able to represent ideas through symbols or rules	A Year 11 class is given the following question. The density of air is 1.3 kg m^3. What mass of air is contained in a room measuring $2.5 \text{ m} \times 4 \text{ m} \times 10 \text{ m}$?

succeeding help is withdrawn. It is through this language of instruction that a student can build on their existing knowledge and understanding. The concept of scaffolding relates to Vygotsky's other key concept of the Zone of Proximal Development. The Zone of Proximal Development incorporates both what the students can do by themselves and what they can do with assistance. It is believed that what students can do today with help in time they will be able to do by themselves. Importantly, Vygotsky stated that the most efficient type of instruction would be aimed at a developmental level just above a student's current level of development. To help us in an understanding of what exactly scaffolding entails imagine the following dialogue relating to Case study 2.1.

Case study 2.1 a Dialogue between Sarah the teaching assistant and Jessica, a student

SARAH: Now, Jessica, choose a parcel. (Jessica picks up the heaviest parcel.) Now tell me, Jessica, is the parcel very heavy or very light?

JESSICA: It is very light.

SARAH (giving Jessica the lightest parcel): Hold this parcel now. Which is the heavier parcel?

JESSICA: They are both light – no, they are both heavy.

SARAH: Now which is it, heavy or light?

JESSICA (pause and mumbles): I don't know.

SARAH: Now what do we mean by heavy? What is heavy?

JESSICA: (Pause.)

SARAH: Have you ever seen an elephant?

JESSICA: Oh yes, I love going to the zoo. Granny took me there last Easter.

SARAH: Could you pick up an elephant?

JESSICA (laughs): Oh no, elephants are too big!

SARAH: So an elephant would be too heavy for you to pick up. Could you pick up a feather?

JESSICA: Feathers are easy to pick up. I love feathers. Granny has feathers in her hat.

SARAH: So a feather is easy to pick up and, well, you couldn't pick up an elephant. So we could say a feather is light and an elephant is heavy. Now what did I say an elephant is? (Waits for Jessica to fill in the rest of the information.)

JESSICA: An elephant is heavy and a feather is light.

SARAH: Good girl! Now hold these two parcels. Which is the heavier and which is the lighter?

JESSICA: (Pauses.)

SARAH: Which is the easier to pick up and which is the harder to pick up?

JESSICA: This is easier to pick up and this one is harder to pick up.

SARAH: If that parcel is the easier to pick up, we could say that the parcel is . . .?

JESSICA: Light.

SARAH: Good girl! So now what is the heavy parcel?

JESSICA: This one, because it is the hardest to pick up.

What this dialogue illustrates is that Jessica needed help to understand the concepts of heavy and light and that this help took the form of carefully selected questions and comments. This example illustrates effective instruction. Effective instruction is not just telling the student what is the right and wrong answer but through language helping them to come to an understanding of the concepts for themselves. This example also shows that when a student is struggling more help is given and when they are succeeding less help is given. You could also say that this example illustrates Piaget's idea of assimilation in that the teaching assistant is trying to have Jessica relate the concepts of heavy and light to what she already knows about elephants and feathers. The difference between Piaget and Vygotsky is that Vygotsky places more emphasis on the language of communication.

Behavioural analysis, task analysis and shaping

As we have mentioned before behaviourists believe that behaviour is controlled by reinforcement (rewards) and punishment. Certainly within school settings we can think of many examples of such from the giving out of stickers or merit points to good old detention.

Feedback and constructive feedback

Feedback from a teacher or teaching assistant depending on the nature of the feedback could be considered as a reward or a punishment. One common type of feedback a teacher or a teaching assistant uses is praise. However, for praise to be effective it must be seen as genuine by the students. For example telling the student that their work is really good when *they* know and *you* know that it isn't, is not very helpful. Perhaps it would be better to focus on one aspect of their work that is good and to praise that. This point leads on to another aspect of giving praise, that is, making it clear to the student what the praise is for. If a student knows what they are being praised for and they find the praise rewarding then they are more likely to repeat that behaviour.

What is often the most difficult aspect of giving feedback is what to say about a student's work when it is clear that they have got completely the wrong idea. **Constructive feedback** is the art of acknowledging what a student has done in a manner that is seen as helpful by the student. Often constructive feedback involves stating something that the student has done well and then focusing on what they need to do next. For example in Case study 2.2 involving the students who were having difficulties coming to grips with essay writing, the teaching assistant could say: 'It is obvious you have spent a lot of effort and time thinking about essay writing but maybe it would be helpful to try it this way.' Such a statement would be an example of constructive feedback. Constructive feedback would *not* be saying to this group of students: 'How many times does the teacher have to explain essay-writing skills, before it sinks in?' Obviously such a statement would only serve to undermine the students' confidence in their own learning.

Analysing behaviour

As we have said before the reason behind giving out rewards and punishments is that rewards should increase a desired behaviour and punishment should decrease an undesired behaviour, but behaviour can be complex as what is a reward or a punishment depends on the individual. According to this theory if a student behaves in a certain way it is because the behaviour gives the student some sort of pay-off. This is true for inappropriate or even very disturbed behaviour. In order to determine why a student behaves in a certain way it is necessary to stand back and observe. In observing behaviour it is important to note:

- What happens before the behaviour. This is sometimes called the antecedent.
- To describe the behaviour.
- To describe the consequences of the behaviour.

Let's examine a case study (1.3) mentioned in Chapter 1, but this time with a few more details.

Time	Antecedent (what happens before the behaviour)	Behaviour	Consequence
10:05	Teacher tells class that they are going to do a mock SAT test		
10:07		James reaches into his pocket and pulls out a beetle, which he puts on his desk	
10:08			Teacher observes the beetle and says, 'James remove that beetle from this class at once'
10:08		James falls on his knees and pleads with the teacher: 'No, sir, this is my best friend, Freddy.	Class are in stitches laughing at what has happened

continued on next page

	I can't go on without Freddy!'	
10:09		The teacher yells: 'Right, James, I have told you before – I will not tolerate you acting up in class. Stand outside right now!'
10:10	James picks up his beetle, smirks and leaves the classroom	

If we look at the consequences of James's behaviour, we see that James escaped from the mock SAT test and received a lot of attention from his peers. We could guess that James finds both these consequences rewarding.

How to change behaviour: shaping and task analysis

Once it has been determined what reinforcement or reward is responsible for a student's behaviour then the teacher needs to consider how to reward appropriate behaviour and how to ignore inappropriate behaviour, keeping in mind what the student finds rewarding. According to this theory to change behaviour you need to shape or reward desired behaviour. However, before you begin to shape new behaviour it is helpful to do what is called a **task analysis**. A task analysis involves looking at a skill which you would like the student to have and breaking that skill into steps or component parts. For example what skills does a student need to have to be able to weigh two objects and decide whether one is heavier than the other? To do this task a student would need to:

• Understand the concepts of heavy and light.
• Be familiar with scales and how to use scales.
• Know how to read the scales and tell how much an object weighs.

Can you think of any more? Perhaps you could break the above steps into even smaller steps.

Let's take another example. What skills does a student need to have in order to be able to successfully write a mock maths SAT test? Certainly they would need:

- To be able to read and understand questions.
- To have relevant information relating to maths stored in their memory. (This step could be further broken down into relevant information on algebra, geometry and so forth.)
- To be able to remember the information when required.

Can you think of any more steps?

If a student can't do a task it is important first to determine what parts of the task they can do and what parts of the task they are having difficulty with. Let us return to the example of James and his beetle. Let us imagine that the reason for James's playing up behaviour is that he knows he can't do the work, but doesn't want others to know that he can't do it. In this case it would be important to first assess what James can do. To use the terminology you would need to carry out a task analysis. Once it has been determined what James can do and what James finds difficult then achievable goals can be set. If James was given realistic goals to work on in class and if he was given praise for achieving these goals, then perhaps he might begin to feel better about being in maths and then maybe he need not act up to escape maths. Over time the expectations of what James can do in maths could be increased slowly at a rate suitable for him, such that in time he could confidently sit and write a mock SAT exam.

Shaping of a behaviour involves starting with a student's existing capabilities and gradually asking more and more of them until they can eventually perform a required task or skill. It is essential for shaping to work, that what is asked of the student at each stage is achievable and that they are rewarded for their achievements. The student must be competent and confident at a previous stage before they can proceed to the next. Shaping is a technique that can be applied to such diverse tasks as tying shoelaces, making toast, doing multiplication, sitting still for twenty minutes and writing an essay.

Multi-sensory approaches

This learning strategy involves teaching a subject in such a way that all senses are being used (Table 2.2). This approach is often used when teaching dyslexic students. This approach is based on the fact that while some people can learn by a variety of means equally well, some have a preferred learning style and some can only learn effectively through one sensory mode. In the case study (2.1) on weighing,

Table 2.2 The senses and their use

Type of learner	Senses used	Examples of preferred learning activities
Kinaesthetic	Touch, movement	Doing things, making models, tracing letters in sand
Visual	Sight	Reading, watching videos
Auditory	Hearing	Listening to tapes, listening to teacher talking

the concept of heavy/light was taught by using the following approaches:

- Touch and movement were used when students had an opportunity to hold parcels to see what was light and what was heavy. Touch and movement were used when students had to put parcels on scales and balance them with multi-link pieces.
- Visual senses were used as the students were watching as the parcels were weighed.
- Auditory senses were used as students were listening to what the teaching assistant and other students had to say.

Specific skills

Questioning

Teachers and teaching assistants will often use questions as a learning support strategy. Questions are asked for a number of reasons including:

- Checking understanding. Finding out what students already know.
- Reviewing and revising previously taught material by recalling to mind what they have previously learned.
- Encouraging thought. Encouraging students to ask questions themselves.
- A way of gaining students' attention. To make sure that students are listening.
- A way of drawing in shyer students.

- A way of finding out why students aren't working as they should.
- To teach a topic through students' answers to questions. (Brown and Wragg 1993)

Work on questioning has revealed that there are different types of question. One dimension of questioning is referred to as *open* versus *closed* or *narrow* versus *broad*. These dimensions describe the types of answer that are required from the student. For example a closed or narrow question would be who is the Prime Minister of the United Kingdom. To that question there is only one answer. On the other hand an open or broad question would be: 'what did you do on your summer holidays?' Obviously here there is no one right answer and the answers given could be quite elaborate. Another dimension of questioning is referred to as *recall* versus *thought*. Recall questions check on existing knowledge and observation, while thought questions stimulate the development of new ideas and in that respect create new knowledge. It is also important to consider whether the questions are clear and easily understood, that is, do the students understand what they are being asked. Also the manner, or tone of voice, in which the questions are asked is important. Are the questions seen as an opportunity to participate in a stimulating classroom discussion or are they a means of catching out those students who are not paying attention? There is an art to questioning, in that there is a need to match the style of the questions to the demands of the lesson and the characteristics of the learner. As we have seen the use of carefully constructed or well thought out questions are an important part of scaffolding. To recap what we have so far learned regarding questions let's look at Table 2.3.

Brown and Wragg (1993) identified a number of common errors in questioning including:

- Asking too many questions.
- Asking a question only to answer it yourself.
- Not giving students enough time to think about the answer to a question.
- Always asking the same students.
- Asking too easy or too difficult questions.
- Not responding to wrong answers.
- Ignoring answers.
- Failing to build on or link students' answers to questions.

Table 2.3 Types of question

Type	Example	Advantage	Disadvantage
Recall narrow	Who is the Prime Minister? Are cats' tails long or short?	Assesses knowledge or observation	Need to match questions to students. If the questions are too simple, the students might appear puzzled as they might think it is a trick, or they might become bored and act up
Recall broad	What did you do in the summer holidays?		
Narrow thought	Do you think the story has a happy ending? Are spiders useful?	Possibility of creating new knowledge	Need to be carefully constructed
Broad thought	How do you think the story will end? What would be the impact on the ecosystem if spiders became extinct?		

Brown and Wragg (1993) outlined a manner of including questions in learning sessions as follows.

Structuring. This involves introducing or explaining the topic of the lesson or support session by asking students questions and expanding on their answers. This could be given to a class of students, a small group or individually. In a sense this sets the scene and tells the students what they are going to be doing.

Pitching and putting. This involves deciding what types of question you are going to ask and when you are going to ask them. Here there is a need to match your questions to the content of the lesson and the characteristics or abilities of your students. For example a question such as: 'What would be the implication on the ecosystem if spiders became extinct?' would be appropriate for Year 10 students, but not reception children. Perhaps a better question for reception students would be: 'Are spiders useful?'

Distributing and directing. This involves deciding who you are going to ask the questions. This avoids only asking the most confident or the brightest. In this way questioning could encourage greater participation; however, care needs to be taken with very shy or withdrawn students. As a teaching assistant you have a role to play here in encouraging responses, as the following example illustrates.

> The Year 7 student I was supporting has no confidence in himself or his abilities and always seems to fear getting something wrong, though I often remind him that it's ok to be wrong. At the end of the lesson the teacher was going through the answers as a class. In turn students were putting their hands up to answer. I approached my student quietly and discreetly and encouraged him to answer the questions. His reply was: 'But what if I am wrong?' I said that he could also be right and once again reminded him that it doesn't matter and pointed out to him that other students were getting it wrong. I then walked away and on the next question the teacher asked, my student reluctantly put his hand half-way up and when asked, he got it right. It was so rewarding to see his face light up. After that there was no stopping him, though he would look over for a little nod of approval from myself.

Pauses and paces. There is an advantage to pausing after a question as this allows students time to think and encourages greater participation. This also avoids the pitfall of overwhelming the students with too many questions.

Prompting or probing. **Prompts** or **probes** are defined as follow-up questions you give students when the answer you get from them is not quite what you are looking for.

Prompts can be made in the following manner:

- Rephrasing the question in simpler language. For example in a literacy session you might initially ask: 'How have the characters developed through this chapter?' If the students look at you with blank expressions you might rephrase the question as: 'How have the characters changed? What were they like at the beginning of the chapter? What were they like at the end?'
- Breaking the initial question into smaller and simpler questions eventually leading back to the initial question. For example during a discussion on the usefulness of spiders in a reception class you might break the question: 'Are spiders useful?' into 'Who has seen a spider?' 'What do spiders do?' and then 'Do you think spiders are useful?'

- Reviewing or reminding students of the information they need to answer the question. For example if you are supporting a student writing an essay on the characteristics of rainforests and the student seems not to know where to begin, you might break the essay into a series of questions that they can answer. One question might be: 'How is a tropical rainforest different from the New Forest, the place where you went on holiday last year?'

Probes are slightly different in that they are additional questions given to try to get the student to give you the more specific information you are looking for. For example if a student replied that spiders are really useful, you might say: 'Well, can you think of an example of how they are useful?'

Listening and responding. Here you need to listen to the students and expand on the students' explanations or ask other students to expand. In this way you are teaching a subject through the questions you give and the answers you receive back. In responding to students' answers you could incorporate other students' previous answers. This is a way of valuing students' contributions as well as reviewing what has been previously said. For example in a discussion on spiders with a small group of students you might say: 'Now John has said that spiders catch flies in their webs and Andy said that he once saw a giant bee caught in a web. So we can agree with Amy that spiders are useful in catching insects.'

Explaining

One stage that could benefit from further comments is how to introduce or explain a topic. Wragg and Brown (1993) suggest:

- Identification of key concepts. For example in starting a learning activity the teacher or teaching assistant will outline to the group or class what they are going to discuss, e.g. 'Today we are going to talk about bears and where they live.' Asking the students what they already know or by reviewing what has been said in previous lessons provides a framework for students to understand new material by connecting it to information they already know.
- Presenting ideas clearly and in a logical order.
- Using language and tone of voice appropriate for the student audience.

- Using a range of strategies to explain key concepts. This could include books, pictures and activities.

Modelling

Bandura in his social learning theory talked about observational learning involving how students watch and learn. Teaching assistants can use this strategy on several levels.

A teaching assistant could shadow other teaching assistants and see what they do and how they relate to students. This is always very useful for the teaching assistant who has just started.

On another level teaching assistants can use the 'watch and learn' approach to show students what they should be doing. They can demonstrate the activity themselves or point out other students who are very good at that skill. For example: 'See how Amy is holding that pencil' or 'Just look at how John turns on his computer' or 'Watch how I am going to add these sums on the white board.'

To encourage good behaviour, a teaching assistant could point out the good behaviour of another student who could serve as a positive role model. Remember what Bandura said about role models – that role models are more effective if the student can relate to them, if the role model is admired and respected by others and if they have seen the role model being rewarded for good behaviour. Take the following example:

> The teacher asked me to hand out the worksheets. One by one I gave out the worksheets. After the tenth child took their sheet, one little boy actually said in a loud voice: 'Thank you, Miss' I immediately replied: 'Well done, Bill! Excellent manners!' and I then gave him a sticker. This caused some sort of impact on the others as they all then thanked me for their work.

On a final note, teaching assistants can act as effective role models for the behaviour which they expect and wish to see in the students they support.

Emotional responses

In the previous chapter we talked about conditioned emotional responses and how for learning to be effective it must not be associated with negative emotions such as fear and anxiety. A teaching assistant can help the student to feel at ease and comfortable in the learning situation. When a student feels emotionally safe, they can take a chance on trying to tackle those subjects they find difficult. If students feel emotionally safe they can risk failure. A key factor in enabling a student to feel emotionally secure and safe is to develop a relationship with the student. But relationships take time as the following examples illustrate:

> Chelsea is incredibly shy and lacks confidence. I knew that to get anywhere with her I first had to gain her trust. I sat next to Chelsea. However, I first asked her if it was ok for me to sit there. She nodded that it was. My first objective was to make her relaxed and happy. I did and said things which I hoped would make her smile. At first I did all the talking, I explained what she needed to do and if Chelsea needed to answer me she would nod or shake her head. Gradually as Chelsea got to know me better she started answering yes or no and finally she started talking normally.

One advantage of having a relationship with someone is that it becomes easier to say those hard things, as one teaching assistant explains:

> I constantly tell my students how I think their work is progressing. I like to use praise and always do so when appropriate. If however they have not worked to their full potential or maybe their behaviour was not appropriate I let them know I was disappointed, as I know they can do better. We talk about why there is a problem and try to solve it together.

Specific strategies

One of the areas that was mentioned in Chapter 2 was a student's awareness of their own memory processes and the strategies that they use to help them learn a task. While more able students just seem to pick these up, students who are struggling could benefit from specific help in such strategies. One such strategy that specifically attempts to teach students how to solve problems systematically is called **process-based instruction** (Ashman and Conway 1993). This strategy aims to teach students how to plan their work. Students are taught to ask themselves a serious of ordered questions. These questions are:

- Where should I start?
- How do I start?
- What is the essential sequence of actions needed? or What steps are involved in completing this assignment?
- Is my plan working as I expected?
- Have I completed the task correctly?
- Have I finished or do I need to go back and do some additional work?

Conclusion

We have covered many strategies. Is there one right one? What strategy is used depends very much on the individual student. In a sense discovering what works and doesn't work is a matter of trial and error and that is where reflection can be very useful.

Reflective component

Case study 2.3: primary school

Jane works with a small group of five Year 4 students on ALS (additional literacy support). Jane completed the following workplace log.

Description of event (What happened? What should have happened?)

I was in the library working with five children on ALS. I first reminded them of the rules of paying attention and that if we want to talk we put our hands up. I told the children we were going to play a game which involved picking a question out of a bag and asking the person next to you that question but we had to answer the question in a complete sentence.

ME: How old are you?
RORY: Eight.
ME: Is that a sentence or a phrase?
RORY: Phrase.

ME: Good. A phrase is just one word that doesn't make complete sense. A sentence begins with a capital letter, ends with a full stop and makes complete sense.

Then we played the game. It went very well that is except for Grace. Grace had real problems with this task. It started when Rory asked Grace a question.

RORY: How many days are there in the week?
GRACE: Seven.
RORY: No, that's a phrase You got it wrong and that was an easy question!

I could see that Grace was looking upset.

ME: Well, Rory, that might be an easy question but it is how you answer that is hard. OK, Rory you ask me a question.

Rory pulled a question out of the bag and asked me what was my favourite meal. I said fish and chips. I deliberately said the wrong answer. The children all laughed, including Grace, and I said, 'See, Rory, this is difficult.' Well, at that point we had to go back to the class.

Feelings (What did I feel? What did the students feel?)

On the whole I felt it went fine, but Grace was having problems with the task. I think I made her feel better by making a mistake myself but that didn't help her with the task.

Evaluation (What was good? What was difficult?)

The children with the exception of Grace all enjoyed the game and by the end really understood the difference between a phrase and a sentence. The difficult part was Grace – she still hadn't a clue.

Analysis (How do I make sense of this? Why did it happen?)

In conclusion (What else could I have done?)

Action plan (Next time I would . . .)

Self-assessment

Your task is to complete the reflective log. Hint: you could refer to Piaget, or task analysis, or scaffolding or the use of questioning as a way forward.

Case study 2.4: secondary school

Let us imagine that we can listen into Donna's (Case study 2.2) session of working with a small group on a set essay. We remember the task is to write an essay comparing the differences between two adverts in terms of form, purpose, audience, content, language and presentation. The session went as follows:

DONNA: When we do an assignment we are going to ask ourselves a series of questions. (Shows group a list of questions, which she had prepared earlier. Each member of the group had a list of these questions. Donna was following the process-based instruction approach.) What is the first question?

SHARON: It says 'Where should I start?' Well, I don't know.

BRAD: My mom always tells me to read the questions first.

DONNA: That's a good idea. It is always a good idea to start off by asking yourself what you are supposed to do.

SHARON: Write an essay about comparing two adverts on the language of persuasion.

DONNA: Yes, that's right. So now let's see what is the next question. 'How do I start?'

SHARON: Well, Miss, that is the hard bit. I don't know what the question even means.

DONNA: Brad, Kim, John, do you have any ideas?

JOHN: I haven't a clue (under his breath) and I couldn't care less.

BRAD: All I know is that I would rather be in Tenerife.

JOHN: Yeah, I'm for that.

DONNA: OK, so would I (everyone laughs) but imagine that if you didn't know anything about Tenerife – how would you know whether you wanted to go there or not?

KIM: I think I get it. It's like deciding where to go at the weekend. If Amy says it's a good place then you know it is, but if my mom thinks I would enjoy it, well, then I would never go there.

DONNA: Yes, that relates to this. In this case the only way we can check out whether the hotel in Tenerife is what we want is by what the advert says.

SHARON: So, Miss, we are supposed to look at the ads and say whether they would convince us whether to go or not. I think I understand now what we are supposed to do. What next, Miss?

DONNA: Now, what's the next question?

BRAD: 'What steps are involved in the assignment?'

DONNA: Well, I would make a plan. In an essay we first need an introduction. An introduction explains what we are going to do, then we need a middle bit, discussing the facts, and then we need the end, where we state our feelings and conclusions.

SHARON: So for the introduction we say we are going to talk about the adverts.

BRAD: It's more than that, we are going to compare adverts.

KIM: So all we have do is just write down what we are going to do.

DONNA: Yes, let's all get out a piece of paper and write that down.

JOHN: What down?

KIM: In this essay we are going to compare adverts on Tenerife.

DONNA: Now that we have got that down what are we going to do next?

SHARON: Miss, we need the middle bit – the facts.

BRAD: Well, this ad talks about a place my parents would go to. I wouldn't be caught dead at a place like that.

DONNA: Why did you say that?

BRAD: Just look at what they say about formal dress for dinner.

DONNA: Well, Brad, that is the type of detail you would need in the middle. After writing all the facts down you need to write a conclusion about what you think of the ads.

TEACHER: Class, you have got two minutes to finish what you are doing.

DONNA: Now I think we have made a good start. If you get stuck with your essay look at the list of questions and we will talk about it next time.

Self-assessment

After reading how the lesson went imagine you are the teaching assistant and write this up as a reflective log. Remember to use the headings.

Chapter 3

Learning styles

Barriers to effective learning

In previous chapters we have discussed potential barriers to learning and ways of overcoming them. Piaget would talk about maturational readiness, that is, a child at a certain age will become able to understand and perform certain academic tasks. So for example, a teacher might explain to a mother of a Year 1 student that the reason her child was having difficulty with reading was that perhaps the child was just not ready, but when they were ready it would just fall into place. Vygotsky, on the other hand, would talk about the importance of matching the language of communication to the child's abilities and level of understanding. For Vygotsky teaching is the art of effective communication. If the explanation is not understandable to the student then learning cannot occur. Other barriers to learning that have been mentioned are the ineffective use of questions, the association of particular classes or subjects with negative emotions such as fear and anxiety and the reinforcement of disruptive and inappropriate behaviour. However, another important characteristic of the student that would affect their ability to learn revolves around what has been described as **learning styles**.

Definitions of learning styles

If you were asked to describe your ideal lesson, what would it be? Would you opt for a stimulating lecture, an audio-visual presentation or a hands-on workshop? Similarly, when you study at home, do you like absolute peace and quiet, some easy-listening background music, or do you prefer to work with the television and radio blaring? What we are talking about here are learning styles. A learning style can be defined as the different and preferred ways in which children and adults think and learn. Though students have their preferred learning styles, often they do not have a choice in regard to how teaching material is presented. Therefore it is just as well that most students, though having preferences in learning styles, can put up with and learn in a variety of situations. However, some students with special educational needs can learn only when information is presented in one way. This is where knowledge regarding learning styles can lead to effective learning support strategies.

Types of learning style

Dunn and Dunn (1993) base the following review of different types of learning style on extensive research.

Preferences in processing information

- *Global versus analytic element.* This refers to how a student prefers to approach a topic. A global approach would see the student preferring to first have an overview of the topic. Globals need to see the big picture before they can concentrate on the details. On the other hand analytics find the whole picture too overwhelming and prefer to approach a topic by starting at the beginning and proceeding step by step in an ordered manner to the conclusion.
- *Impulsive versus reflective element.* This refers to the amount of time a student takes to think about a task before they start to work. Some students prefer to take their time and seriously consider the task before they begin. The difficulty with this approach is that while the student thinks about the task nothing is actually written down. This can be discouraging both to the student and to the teacher. At the other extreme some students don't even take time to read the instructions properly; they just jump in. Obviously students at both extremes will have difficulty successfully completing the task. Perhaps teachers or teaching assistants need to encourage a certain amount of thinking and planning time before the student starts to write.

Environmental learning styles

- *Preferences in regard to sound or background noise.* Here individuals would differ in regard to what level of noise they found most helpful when learning or studying.
- *Preferences in regard to room temperature.* Again some individuals will prefer a cool room, while others prefer a warm or hot environment.
- *Preferred classroom design.* This relates to preferences for seating arrangements. Do you prefer to study sitting in a traditional desk and chair? Do you prefer a more informal environment of chairs and tables being arranged in groups or a semi-circle? Do you prefer learning while sitting on a couch, or on the floor?
- *Preferred level of lighting.* This dimension states that there are preferences in regard to soft, dim or bright lights.

The teacher can to some extent control factors such as noise levels, room temperature, lighting and classroom design. These factors have an important role to play in supporting learning for students with autism, ADHD and dyslexia. (See Chapter 4 for further discussion.)

Emotional learning styles

- *Degree of responsibility preferred.* Does the student prefer to work independently *without any* adult supervision, feedback or guidance? Does the student prefer to have *some* adult supervision, feedback and guidance? Does the student prefer *frequent* adult supervision, feedback and guidance? This is an area that has particular relevance to teaching assistants. Of course the key here is knowing the students you work with. For example, a teaching assistant might state the following:

> Well Sarah (a Year 9 student) always wants me to sit right beside her. Now John (Year 9, in a different class) hates me sitting beside him. It took me a while to figure John out. When I sat next to him he wouldn't even look at me and he just mumbled 'Yes' or 'No' to my questions. Now I sit at the back and John and I have this system. When he looks at me, I know he wants me to come and help him, but I only go to his desk if I see him looking at me. It's all about 'street cred'. We get on great now, as John knows that I am there if he needs me.

- *Degree of structure preferred.* This refers to student preferences in regard to structured learning activities and tasks. Does the student want to be told in precise detail what the learning task is and exactly how they should do it or does the student prefer to be given choices in both what to do and how to do it? Again it seems that knowing the preferences of the student whom you are supporting is important.
- *Degree of persistence individuals bring to educational task.* The level of persistence a student brings to a task depends on the student's attention span, ability and interest. Some students will prefer to work on one task at a time, preferring to finish one task before they move on to the next, while some students like to have many tasks on the go at the same time.
- *Degree of motivation individuals bring to educational task.* This refers to the degree to which a student is interested in learning at school. Some students will be self-motivated. They have a deep internal need to learn. Motivation to learn in this case is said to be **intrinsic**. Some students are motivated to learn only if the subject interests them. Some students' motivation to go to school is that they can be near their friends. For these students feedback and praise from their friends are an important source of motivation. Knowing what motivates a student to learn can have practical applications. For example, a teaching assistant might say:

> Sam [Year 1 student] just did not like to read, or at least he didn't seem to like to read from the books we were using in class. Then his mom mentioned to the teacher that he was particularly interested in stars and black holes. Well, the teacher and I searched the library for all the books we could find on these topics. Sam still has to read the books from the reading scheme, but now, as a reward for finishing his class book, the next book we read is one of his choosing.

In this example Sam's motivation to learn about stars and black holes was used to develop reading.

Preferences in social patterns

This learning style refers to whether a student prefers to:

- Work alone.

- Work as a member of a pair or small group/large group.
- Work with adult supervision.
- Have variety in regard to whom they work with *or* take comfort in set routines and work patterns.

Of course all these preferences may vary from class to class or from subject to subject.

Physiological learning style

- *Perceptual style: visual, auditory or kinaesthetic learner.* This approach states that students prefer to be taught and learn more when the teaching activities match their **perceptual style**. Perceptual style refers to how students take in and process information. Specifically we are looking at what senses (e.g. sight, sound, touch) are being used to process information.

  - **Visual learners** prefer teaching activities which involve seeing and watching. This type of student will learn by watching demonstrations, videos, or by looking at pictures, maps and diagrams.
  - **Auditory learners** prefer teaching activities that involve hearing and listening. Such students will learn best by listening to tapes, lectures or music.
  - **Kinaesthetic learners** learn through physical movement and touching. Such students would prefer hands-on activities.

  Though most individuals will have one main perceptual style it is possible to have different perceptual styles depending on the task involved. The following questions according to Rose (1987) can help identify your perceptual style.

  When you spell:

  (a) Do you try to visualise or see the word in your mind?
  (b) Do you sound out the word, that is, break the word into individual sound units?
  (c) Do you need to write the word down to see if it feels right?

  When you read:

  (a) Do you see images in your mind?
  (b) Do you enjoy reading plays? Do you hear the characters talking in your head?

(c) Are the only books you read action stories, or 'how to' books? Would you rather do things than read?

When you are putting something together:

(a) Do you need to look at the directions and diagrams?
(b) Do you need to have someone tell you what to do, step by step?
(c) Do you skip the directions and just figure it out as you go along?

Scoring

If you answered (a) you are a visual learner.
If you answered (b) you are an auditory learner.
If you answered (c) you are a kinaesthetic/tactile learner.

- *Time of day.* Most people will feel they work better at certain times. Some people will say they are morning people, while others feel they are at their best very late in the evening. However, most of the decisions in regard to what subject is taught when will be made by the teacher or on a school level.
- *Food and drink intake.* This refers to an individual's preference to eat or drink when they are studying. Many people will say that they feel they can concentrate better when they have had a cup of coffee. Some individuals feel they study better when they are eating or chewing something. However, most schools will have strict rules of conduct regarding these issues.
- *Need for mobility or moving around.* This refers to an individual's preference for moving their body while being involved in a learning task. Sometimes a student is not aware of the degree to which they are moving or fidgeting. These individuals might say that fidgeting actually helps them concentrate. However, another student might say that having someone next to them puts them off studying. Some students prefer to sit still while learning and studying. Again schools will have rules concerning students' obligation to remain in their seats.

Adapting learning support strategies to accommodate different types of learning style

An individual's learning style is of interest to teachers and teaching assistants for a number of reasons. If a student is not learning it could be that the way information is presented does not match their preferred learning style.

As a teacher or teaching assistant you might look at this information and say, 'Great! All we need to do is figure out a student's learning style and then teach them accordingly.' This sounds a good idea. But like many good ideas applying this knowledge to the classroom is not without its difficulties.

In this chapter many types of learning style have been described. Therefore if we tried to describe an individual student's learning style taking in as many types as possible it could be quite complex. For example we might find that Jason:

- Has a visual learning style for spelling.
- Is somewhat impulsive, that is, he tends to start tasks without fully understanding what he has to do.
- Is an analytical learner, that is, he likes to learn step by step.
- Prefers a hot, brightly lit classroom.
- Prefers frequent adult supervision.
- Has a need to move or fidget constantly.

Of course this becomes more complex as we would need to measure every student's learning style. And if every student had their own unique preferred way of learning, how would it be possible to meet everyone's needs at the same time? At best what most teachers/teaching assistants can do is to teach using a variety of approaches, therefore pleasing some of the students at least some of the time.

The question also arises as to whether some learning styles are better than others. Certainly as children progress through the school system teaching seems to favour learners who can sit quietly at their seats and take in information which is presented in a traditional auditory format. So you could say that it would be good for students to have to learn in many ways as it would prepare them for life, where they cannot always choose the manner in which they have to learn.

However, as previously stated, learning style theory becomes more important when working with students with special educational needs, who might have the ability to learn in only one particular way. If this is the case then it is essential to find out what the student's learning style is. But how are learning styles measured? Traditionally learning styles have been measured by asking students to answer questions regarding how they like to learn. The problem with this approach is that some students with special educational needs might not have the ability to answer the questions or the awareness of how they learn best. In this case the best way forward, for a teacher/teaching assistant, is to observe the student's behaviour in a variety of learning situations (e.g. working in groups versus working alone, having frequent adult help versus being left alone to get on with it, or having visual, auditory, kin-aesthetic activities) and make notes regarding which conditions result in the most effective learning.

Reflective component

Case study 3.1: special school

Judy works at a school for children with mild and moderate learning disabilities. She works as a teaching assistant supporting children in developing life skills.

Description of event (What happened? What should have happened?)

Today I was working in the kitchen supporting students learning about food technology. Today's task was for the students to make sausage rolls. In doing this they would need to use the food processor to make the pastry. After the students had weighed the ingredients we read through the recipe together. I explained that the flour needed to be processed for about five seconds. I then told the pupils that the margarine should be cut into small pieces, added to the flour and processed for about ten seconds. I showed the pupils ten seconds on the timer. I explained that water should then be added a few drops at a time and the mixture should be processed until it became a ball of pastry in the bowl. I checked that the students under-stood the instructions by having them repeat them back to me. They both did this with some help and then they went back to their respec-tive kitchens with a copy of the instructions.

Now, of the two pupils I was working with, Sidney has problems with reading and sometimes difficult behaviour. The other pupil, Joe, has mild learning disabilities but is quite good at reading. I thought that of the two Sidney would have the most problems in following the recipe, so I stayed with him and watched to make sure he carried out the instructions. Contrary to what I thought he actually did very well and achieved the required result of a good ball of pastry.

I then moved on to the second pupil, Joe (the very able reader). Upon looking in his bowl I realised that he had not followed the instructions but had combined all his ingredients together with too much water. Joe seemed very upset and said he hated cooking. I told him not to worry because the problem could be put right by adding some more flour before rolling out the pastry. In the end the sausage rolls were cooked and thoroughly enjoyed by both boys.

Feelings (What did I feel? How do I think the students felt?)

In the end we got there and I think the students enjoyed the activity. However, Joe was quite upset with the state of his pastry.

Evaluation (What was good? What was difficult?)

The students were involved in the learning. This was very much a hands-on activity, what Piaget would see as discovery learning. I feel I did not keep an adequate eye on both boys. I did, however, learn from this experience that whilst Joe is very good at reading he does not have the ability to use his reading skills to help him follow instructions.

Analysis (How do I make sense of this? Why did this happen?)

Well, from what I know about learning styles I would say that Joe could prefer to have frequent adult supervision.

In conclusion (What else could I have done?)

I could have stayed with Joe and let Sidney work by himself, or perhaps I could have worked with them both together.

Action plan (Next time I would . . .)

Next time I need to give more attention to Joe.

Self-assessment

1 How would you describe Joe's and Sidney's learning styles?
2 What other possible explanations could there be for Joe's difficulties in the kitchen?
3 How would you complete the analysis, conclusion and action plan of this reflective log?

Chapter 4

Pupils with special needs

Definitions of special needs

When working in a school a number of children will be identified as having special educational needs. The 1981 Education Act has defined a child as having special educational needs if:

- S/he has significantly greater difficulty in learning than the majority of the children of her/his age; or
- S/he has a disability, which either prevents or hinders her/him from making use of the educational facilities of a kind generally provided in schools within the area of the local authority concerned for children of his age.

(Cited in Daniels *et al.* 1999)

This definition is very broad and will include children who have been diagnosed as having **dyslexia, dyspraxia, autism, ADHD**, communication disorders, **Down's syndrome** or physical/sensory impairments. However, even if two children have the same diagnosis the degree or extent to which they have the condition will often differ.

A further complication is that often a child will not have one condition but a combination of conditions. When a child has a combination of conditions experts talk about **co-morbidity**, that is, the degree to which one condition is associated with another. For example, a child might have a dual diagnosis of dyslexia and ADHD with autistic tendencies. *Tendencies* is another term used by experts when a child will have some aspects of that condition but not enough to warrant a diagnosis.

In any discussion of diagnosis it is important to remember that a child is first and foremost an individual with his/her own personality.

What all of this means for adults supporting children with special needs is that every child is unique and each child will have their own distinctive profile of strengths and weaknesses. This awareness needs to be considered when looking at recommended teaching and learning support strategies. It would be nice to be able to say that if a child has dyslexia or autism, then just try this approach and they will learn. However, for the reasons listed above, it is not always that simple. A strategy that will work with one child might not work equally well with another child even though the two children have the same condition.

This chapter aims to describe briefly various special needs and corresponding learning support and teaching strategies that have been found to be effective. When as a teaching assistant you are working with students with special educational needs, you will very much be working under the direction of the teacher and the Special Educational Needs Co-ordinator (Senco). Therefore communication and dialogue between all those involved is crucial. In order to monitor the progress of a student, records need to be kept regarding what strategies have been tried and to what success. As a teaching assistant, your detailed observations and comments regarding what happens during a learning support session will be an important contribution to these records.

Before going on it is important to say a few words about IQ or **intelligence tests.** IQ tests are often used by educational psychologists as part of the process of diagnosing specific educational needs. The following shows the correspondence between educational label and IQ score (Atkinson *et al.* 1993).

Educational label	IQ score
Very superior	130+
Superior	120–9
High average	110–19
Average	90–109
Low average	80–9
Borderline	70–9
Mild learning disabilities	55–69
Moderate learning disabilities	40–54
Severe learning disabilities	25–39
Profound learning disabilities	0–24

Autistic Spectrum Disorder (autism and Asperger's)

Today psychologists and psychiatrists use two classification systems in order to determine whether someone has autistic disorder or Asperger's disorder. The classification systems are the *Diagnostic and Statistical Manual* (*DSM* IV) and the *International Classification of Diseases* (*ICD* 10). These classification systems set out the behaviour an individual has to show in order to receive a certain diagnosis.

The difference between autism and Asperger's has been widely debated. Some will argue that Asperger's is the more able end of the autistic spectrum, while others will argue that it is a very different condition. The *DSM* IV states that in contrast to autism, there are no clinically significant delays in language communication and cognitive development with Asperger's disorder (APA 1995, p. 78).

Since the 1980s many professionals when referring to autism and Asperger's will use the phrase Autistic Spectrum Disorder, ASD for short. This phrase reflects the fact that individuals diagnosed with this condition will differ greatly in terms of ability. At one end of the spectrum you will have an individual with no language and profound learning disabilities, while at the other end the individual will have an average IQ and a good command of language.

So far ASD has been described in the technical language used by psychologists and psychiatrists. However, what do these diagnostic criteria mean in practice?

The sorts of problems that might occur when supporting such pupils and what a teacher or teaching assistant might notice

The following illustrates what characteristics or problems a student with autism or Asperger's might show that a teacher or teaching assistant might notice. Remember, depending on where they are within the autistic spectrum, individuals will differ in regard to the characteristics they demonstrate.

Problems in social interaction

- Reluctance to maintain eye contact.
- Child not being able to make sense of, or understand, body language and facial expressions.

- Child will fail to develop age-appropriate friendships.
- A child will not share his/her interests with others. A young child will often share his/her interest in an object by pointing to that object. (e.g. child points to a big bus as if to say 'Look at that bus'). A child with ASD will not do this.
- A child will lack empathy. The child will not understand, be able to interpret, or respond to another person's emotional reactions. If a child with ASD accidentally pushes another child over, he/she will not understand why the other child is upset or angry with them.
- A child will not realise that as they have their own unique thoughts and feelings, so do other people. A child will not have a theory of mind. (See p. 27.)
- A child will be confused by social situations.

Problems in communication and imaginative activity

- A child could have no language or be delayed in language development. The child does not try to make up for problems in language development by the use of facial expressions and body language.
- If the child does have language, there could be problems in starting and sustaining conversations. Such conversations will often break social rules (e.g. a student might ask the Head Teacher why his breath smells).
- A child might use repetitive phrases (i.e. jingle bells) that they have learned from others or from watching television. The key point here is that these phrases are not used to communicate with others but are spoken as the child simply likes the sound of the phrase.
- A child might have a wide vocabulary but have a tendency to take things literally. (e.g. If someone says it is raining cats and dogs, then they might be looking to see where the cats and dogs are.)
- Lack of spontaneous make-believe play. The play of children with ASD is very different. Children with ASD will often line toys up. Sometimes they can become fixated on one toy or object.

Limited range of activities and interests

- An all-consuming preoccupation with one or more restricted areas of interest that is abnormal in its intensity or focus. Many individuals have hobbies, but in individuals with ASD the hobby or interest can become an obsession. For example: a small boy who becomes fascinated with vacuum cleaners, knows everything there is to know about vacuum cleaners and will, if given a chance, talk about nothing else but vacuum cleaners.

- Keeping to routines or rituals is extremely important. If routines are broken this will lead to great distress. For example: at 10:45 we go out for our break. We can't go out for break at 10:30 as it is not the right time. The right time is 10:45.
- Repetitive motor mannerisms. This can take the form of hand-flapping, clapping or rocking backwards and forwards.

How to deal with these problems

Lack of eye contact

Suggested strategy. Do not expect eye contact and never turn their face to look at you (*Special Children*, 2001b, p. 37).

Obsession with routines

Suggested strategies. A structured environment, with specific areas for specific tasks and an area for individual work and personal space is recommended. Treatment and Education of Autistic and related Communications-handicapped Children (TEACCH) is widely used within schools. The TEACCH approach (Mesibov 2003) talks about the culture of autism and the need for structure. Structure is important to an individual with autism as change is seen as frightening. A rigid routine will allow the student with autism to be able to predict to a certain extent what is going to happen next. If a student feels secure in the routine, then hopefully they will begin to feel comfortable and relaxed. At this stage they then will be able to learn. If a child with autism has problems in communication it is suggested that routines be indicated by visual aids. One aid could be the use of a visual timetable, which is constantly available to the child. If a child has not developed the ability to tell the time by looking at a watch or a clock, a large adapted hourglass or egg-timer could be used to indicate to the child when it is time to move on to the next activity.

Lack of understanding of how to react in social situations

Suggested strategy: social stories. The social story approach developed by Carol Gray (1994) aims to describe a situation which the child finds personally difficult. As this approach focuses on the telling of a story, it is designed for the more able child with ASD. It is important that the story is written in a language that matches the child's level of understanding. There are formulas for writing such stories. These include:

- *Descriptive sentences.* These sentences describe exactly what happens, where it happens and why it happens. The reasons for participating in the activity are given. In day-to-day life there are many un-written and unspoken rules regarding social expectations and codes of behaviour. These unwritten and unspoken rules need to be specifically pointed out and explained to a child with ASD. These descriptive sentences should include terms such as *usually* or *sometimes* rather than always. The use of such words will help a child with ASD deal with unexpected changes to the routines.
- *Perspective sentences.* These sentences describe the responses, re-actions and feelings of other people in a situation. A child with ASD will not understand why other people do what they do and in this respect will benefit from such information.
- *Directive sentences.* These sentences often take the form of gentle advice. For example: 'I will try to do this' (Rowe 1999; Smith 2001).

The following is an example of a social story. In this example Jason finds sitting in the school assembly difficult. When the other children talk and shout, Jason becomes visibly upset and screams at them to be quiet. Sometimes Jason becomes so angry, he has to be removed from the assembly.

Jason's story: Going to assembly

My name is Jason.

I am a pupil at Crossroads village school.

A lot of other boys and girls go to our school.

Usually Mrs Robinson teaches my class and Miss Philips helps me with my work.

Usually the whole school goes to assembly every morning.

Usually we go to assembly after the teacher has taken the register.

When we are in assembly we are supposed to sit quietly.

Sometimes children can be very noisy. Sometimes children can make a lot of noise moving their chairs.

When the other children make noise it is up to the teachers and other helpers to ask them to be quiet.

I will try to ignore the noise the other children are making

I should try to sit quietly in assembly.

If I sit quietly everyone will be very pleased with me.

My teachers will all say, 'Isn't Jason good?' 'Jason is a good boy for behaving so well in assembly.'

Dyslexia

Individuals with dyslexia will have difficulties with words. Critchley (1970, p. 11) defined dyslexia as 'a disorder manifested by difficulty in learning to read, despite conventional instruction, adequate intelligence and socio-cultural opportunity'. Therefore in order to diagnose dyslexia an educational psychologist must rule out the following:

• Overall low intelligence.
• Lack of schooling.
• A socially disadvantaged background that did not provide the child with opportunities to read and enjoy books.
• Hearing or visual difficulties.
• Emotional or behavioural problems that might influence the child's ability to learn.

Not surprisingly it often takes time for dyslexia to be diagnosed. Dyslexia is seen as a discrepancy between the child's general ability and the child's performance on reading and spelling tests. What teachers or teaching assistants will notice is that an apparently very bright child is just not progressing at reading and spelling.

The sort of problems that might occur when supporting such pupils and what a teacher or teaching assistant might notice

Poor auditory short-term memory

• Inability to carry out a sequence of instructions.
• Forgetting what he/she was going to say in the middle of a sentence or a conversation.
• Problems in remembering what was given for homework.

Difficulties in language/speech

- Late speech development.
- Confusion between similar sounds in speech, e.g. f, th, v.
- Inability to recognise rhymes.

Problems with visual processing

- Difficulties in co-ordinating binocular vision, which results in the child feeling that the words on the page are moving.
- Over-sensitivity to light or glare that would make reading difficult.

Difficulties in sequencing and organising

- Difficulty in learning the days of the week, months of the year.
- Difficulty in organising ideas.
- Difficulty in organising notes for study and revision.

Difficulties in phonological awareness

- Inability to remember sound/letter (symbol) associations, i.e. what sounds go with which letters.
- Difficulty in blending letter sounds together to form words.
- A bizarre spelling as a result of not knowing which letters correspond to which sounds.

Over-reliance on phonics

Here we see that not all individuals with dyslexia will have the same pattern of difficulties. These individuals seem to understand sound/letter associations but tend to make errors in treating *irregular* words as *regular* words. For example a student might read 'island' as 'izland' or they might spell 'island' as 'iland'.

Poor sense of direction

Confusion between left and right.

Clumsiness

Individuals who have dyslexia have a higher risk of also having dyspraxia (*Special Children*, 2000c; Pascal 2002).

It is important to note that students with dyslexia will differ in regard to the severity of the condition and the reasons underlying their difficulties. For example some students might have reading and spelling difficulties due to problems with visual processing. Other students could have difficulties due to problems with phonological awareness or perhaps an over-reliance on phonics. The fact that dyslexia has a number of causes is an important one as the teaching/learning support strategy needs to take into account the reasons for the students' difficulties.

How to deal with these problems

It is helpful to note that the following strategies are useful for both students who have been diagnosed with dyslexia and students who are experiencing difficulties with reading and spelling.

Multi-sensory techniques

Multi-sensory techniques involve the teaching of phonics through an approach that uses all senses, that is, auditory, visual, kinaesthetic and tactile (Thomson 1990). For example a student would be taught through the following approaches.

- *Auditory approaches.* The student hears the word and would be required to repeat the word.
- *Visual approaches.* Here the student sees the printed word. Sometimes students can look in a mirror when reading words so they can see how their lips and tongue form the sounds. Sometimes students can be encouraged to see or visualise the word on the wall and then copy it down.
- *Tactile/kinaesthetic.* The student writes the word. Using joined-up writing is helpful as it encourages the hand to remember the sequence of movements. Sometimes the students are encouraged to feel the word as it is presented to them in three-dimensional letters. Alternatively students could trace the letters in the sand or on someone's back. Running around big shapes and letters in the playground establishes a whole-body feel for the shapes involved (*Dyslexia in the Primary Classroom* 1997; Pascal 2002).

Memory techniques

For words that students find difficult it is suggested that they make up stories to help remember them, for example, 'Sister Alice is dizzy' stands for 'said'.

Hardwick (1996) suggests the use of personalised flashcards. On one side of the flashcard the student writes the word they find difficult. On the other side they write a personally meaningful sentence including that word. For example on one side of the flashcard is the target word 'believe' and on the other side is written: 'I want to believe' accompanied by a picture of a UFO. Or imagine the target word is 'never'. On one side is the word 'never' and on the other side is written 'you will never make me talk' with an accompanying picture of a spy.

Structured programmes

There are many programmes that exist to teach the skills of spelling. Some programmes concentrate on a phonics approach, that is, learning systematically the rules associating letters with sounds. Other programmes focus on more visual approaches such as encouraging the student to recognise words within words. For example *damage* is composed of two words *dam* and *age*. Regardless of what teaching/learning support strategy is used with the student, a key role of the teaching assistant working with such a student would be to pay close attention to how the student progresses and to record this information. Important information to record would include not only what words the student got *right*, but also what words they got *wrong*. It is important to record how the student writes the word as an analysis of spelling mistakes might reveal clues to underlying difficulties.

The following is a short case study involving a teaching assistant working with a student with dyslexia.

Case study 4.1

Valerie, a teaching assistant in a Year 3 class, was working with Sonia. Sonia, though a bright young child, struggled with reading and spelling. Valerie was reading a book entitled *Biff and Chip go to the Moon*. Sonia had been on the same book for the last two days but was still having difficulty with most of the words. Sonia struggled through the first two pages and then said that she was fed up with the book and that she wasn't going to read any more.

On a very practical level there are certain things that Valerie could do to help Sonia with her reading.

- If a child is having great difficulty sounding out a word, step in and give a suitable prompt to the student. For example if the student got stuck on the word 'climb' say the first part of the word, i.e. 'cli', then if necessary complete the word. The key point is not to let frustration build up.
- Share the reading. You, the teaching assistant, read one line, the student can read the next. Sometimes using funny voices can help motivate younger students.
- Every now and then stop and talk about what has happened and what you think will happen next. This encourages comprehension. Perhaps the student can use these clues about what should happen next to help him/her sound out the words.
- Perhaps, as a break from reading the required text on the reading scheme, the student can read a book of their own choice. The key point is that the activity of reading is enjoyable.

(Pascal 2002)

Dyspraxia

Dyspraxia, or **Developmental Co-ordination Disorder** (as it is called in the *DSM* IV), refers to problems in motor co-ordination experienced by a child that cannot be explained by a general medical condition and that such problems result in the child being substantially behind their peers in motor milestones. Problems in motor co-ordination can effect both gross and fine motor skills. In some individuals the motor movements effected also include the mouth and the tongue, resulting in problems with speech. These problems in motor co-ordination are thought to result from an immaturity in the way in which the brain processes information.

Theorists (Conrad *et al.* 1983) talk of two aspects of dyspraxia. These aspects are **ideational** dyspraxia and **ideo-motor** dyspraxia.

- *Ideational dyspraxia* refers to difficulties with planning a sequence of co-ordinated movement. These children might always put their socks and shoes on before their trousers.

- *Ideo-motor dyspraxia* on the other hand refers to individuals who know what they want to do, know what the right sequence of actions is, but somehow their body does not do what they want it to. These individuals appear awkward and clumsy.

The sort of problems that might occur when supporting such pupils and what a teacher or teaching assistant might notice

Fine motor problems

- Messy handwriting, poor copying skills, immature drawings.
- Lack of secure tripod grip of pen/pencil.
- Difficulty in dressing most noticeable in PE. Difficulties with fastening buttons, doing shoelaces up, etc. Always the last to get changed.
- Great difficulties in using scissors.
- Difficulties with assembling puzzles. Avoids construction toys.
- Messy eaters.

Gross motor problems

- Poor posture, awkward movements.
- Poor PE skills, difficulties in running, hopping, climbing, balancing and catching or kicking a ball.

Poor spatial awareness

- Tendency to bump into objects or people.
- Tendency to drop objects, or knock things over as individuals seem to have difficulty in being aware of how close their hands are, *or* need to be, to objects.
- Tendency to get too close to others, right in your face.

Poor auditory and visual short-term memory

- Poor listening skills.
- Difficulties in following sequential instructions. If given a series of three instructions, e.g. 'Put your name on your work,' 'Put your work on my desk' and then 'Put your chair on the table,' the

dyspraxic child might put their chair on the table but in doing so forget the other two instructions.

• Difficulty in copying words from the board.

No laterality or lack of bilateral integration (inability to integrate both sides of the body)

• No clearly dominant hand. Sometimes they will write with their right hand and sometimes they will write with their left.

• The child will use the right hand to do tasks on the right side of their body and will use their left hand to do tasks on the left side of their body.

Organisational skills

Poorly developed organisational skills, e.g. remembering what to bring to school, what homework needs to be completed, what class you should be in. Especially a problem in secondary school.

Problems in social esteem

The above difficulties can lead to the individual being isolated, friendless and ridiculed (*Special Children* 2000a; Ripley *et al.* 1997).

How to deal with these problems

The first point to make is that those children who are dyspraxic need to be recognised as such and not just labelled as awkward or clumsy.

It is suggested that programmes of activities which focus on gross and fine motor movements be practised on a daily basis. These programmes often include practising a good upright posture, balance, jumping, and finger exercises and cross lateral exercises, that is, touching right knee with left hand. Such exercises are developed on an individual basis with input from physiotherapists. Often teaching assistants are involved in implementing such programmes.

Aside from these programmes involving practising physical activities there are a number of practical steps that can be taken to help the dyspraxic student. Let's look at the following case study written from the perspective of the student.

Case study 4.2: John's story

I arrive late in class. I have forgotten my book bag again! Miss is cross. I can't sit down as I have no chair. I walk over to get one, but I fall over Tom's feet and in the process knock down the new science display! Miss is not pleased! Everyone laughs at me!

It is the literacy hour. Miss reads a story. But I find it hard to follow as I find it hard to keep still. Billy complains to the teacher that I keep bumping him. I don't do it on purpose, it just happens. After Miss has finished the story I go back to my seat and am told to copy the words from the board. I find this difficult! My pencil is broken and every time I sharpen it breaks again. Everyone on my table has finished copying the words and I haven't started. I have to stay in at break and finish copying the words.

After break it is time for numeracy. We are playing with the Mental Maths Monkey. James throws me the monkey and I am supposed to catch it and answer the question $2 + 2 = ?$ I am happy, as I know the answer, but I miss catching the monkey and it lands in the fish tank. When I try to get the monkey out of the fish tank I catch a fish and hurt it I don't mean to.

It is lunchtime. No one wants to sit next to me as they say I make such a mess and that I look disgusting when I eat. I am not looking forward to the afternoon as we have PE.

What this case study illustrates is how difficult the school day can be for a student with dyspraxia. However, there are ways in which the day could be made easier. With knowledge of the kind of things that John finds difficult, the teacher and teaching assistant could make the day easier. A teaching assistant could ensure that John has a seat that he can easily get to when he arrives in the class. A teaching assistant could be on hand to provide John with some pencils that have already been sharpened. The teacher could write on the board with different coloured pens for every line. Alternatively John could have a copy of the words beside him. John could be given extra time to complete his work or be given a target (number of words that he can copy) that he can achieve. It is important that John not be put in situations where he will fail. Instead of throwing the Mental Maths Monkey, the monkey could be passed around. Most important, John needs praise and lots of praise to boost his self-esteem.

Down's syndrome

In 1959 Down's syndrome was identified as a chromosomal disorder, instead of there being forty-six chromosomes in each cell, there are forty-seven. Later the extra chromosome was identified as a partial or an extra chromosome 21; thus sometimes Down's syndrome is referred to as Trisomy 21. While there are common traits similar to all individuals with Down's syndrome there are great variations in terms of ability between individuals. It is now not uncommon for individuals with Down's syndrome to be included in mainstream education, for children to belong to cubs or brownies and for adults to hold jobs within the community.

The sort of problems that might occur when supporting such pupils and what a teacher or teaching assistant might notice

Hearing

Doesn't seem to be listening. Figures suggest that as many as 40 per cent of individuals with Down's syndrome have mild hearing loss with 15 per cent having severe hearing loss. Hearing tests are essential for individuals with Down's syndrome.

Limited auditory short-term memory

- Difficulty listening to and following complex instructions.
- Might repeat the last part of what you have said to them. This might be the only part of the sentence that they have heard and remembered. In this case you might need to repeat what you have just said.

Thinking, reasoning and generalising knowledge to new situations

An individual might learn how to add 20 + 5 but have problems adding a new sum.

Delayed motor skills, fine and gross

As in dyspraxia, there could be difficulties with fine movement, e.g. handwriting, using eating utensils, doing up buttons and with gross skills such as running and jumping.

Problems in speech production

What is said can be hard to understand due to problems in pronunciation.

Past problems with low expectations

In the past, society has assumed that Down's syndrome individuals had limited capabilities. Up to 1979 it was the opinion of professionals that individuals with Down's syndrome were incapable of learning to read, therefore they were never taught. However, more recent research (Buckley and Bird 1993) has revealed that with the right teaching approach many Down's syndrome children can learn to read (Buckley and Bird 1993; Buckley 1995; *Special Children* 2001a).

Though Down's syndrome individuals have difficulties in certain areas they also have strengths. In individuals with Down's syndrome the visual memory may be more effective than auditory memory. Though individuals with Down's syndrome might have difficulty expressing themselves through spoken communication they are often very good at picking up and interpreting body language and facial expressions and making their feelings and thoughts known through non-verbal communication.

How to deal with these problems

- Keep instructions short and simple. If instructions are too long an individual with a limited short-term memory will only remember a small part of what is said.
- Use familiar language. Always check for understanding before proceeding with a task.
- When teaching new skills make the most of visual material.
- As individuals with Down's often have difficulty in speech pronunciation you will need to listen carefully.

- Set realistic targets.
- Practise fine and gross motor skills.

(Special Children 2001a)

Case study 4.3

Amy was working with John, a Down's syndrome student, in Year 7. Recently Amy had attended a training day on supporting students with Down's syndrome. Amy decided to use her newly acquired knowledge to help her plan a learning support session with John on the recognition of money. This is what Amy planned to do.

- Lay real coins on a table, 50p, 20p, 10p and 5p.
- Point to coins, asking John what they were.
- Ask John to select a certain coin and state what it was.
- Once confident with the task, move the lesson to the vending machine in the cafeteria.

  John could choose an item that he wished to have. He then needed to select the correct money and decide which coin went into which slot. If John was correct he could keep the chosen item as a reward.

Amy reported that the lesson went very well and led to John having greater confidence with money both inside and outside of school.

ADHD

The *DSM* IV (APA 1995) describes three types of attention disorder:

- Attention Deficit/Hyperactivity Disorder, predominantly inattentive type.
- Attention Deficit/Hyperactivity Disorder, predominantly hyperactive-impulsive.
- Attention Deficit/Hyperactivity Disorder, combined type.

Most children at some points will have problems with paying attention, being over-active and difficulties resulting from acting without thinking. But what marks individuals with this disorder as different from your average child is the degree to which they have problems in these areas and how these difficulties influence all aspects of their lives.

The sort of problems that might occur when supporting such pupils and what a teacher or teaching assistant might notice

Inattention

- Makes careless mistakes in schoolwork often resulting from not paying close attention to detail.
- Difficulty in staying on task.
- Often does not listen when spoken to.
- Often fails to complete an activity.
- Problems with organisation. Often loses things and forgets to bring the right equipment to class.
- Easily distracted.

Hyperactivity

- Can't keep still, constantly fidgeting.
- Even though instructed to remain seated will constantly leave seat to move around.
- Runs or climbs excessively in situations which are inappropriate.
- Finds it difficult to participate in quiet pastimes.
- Constantly talking.

Impulsiveness

- Blurts out answers without waiting to be asked.
- Acts without considering the consequences; acts first, thinks later.
- Difficulty in awaiting turns.
- Interrupts conversations or games.

Problems in relating to others

Peers will often find these children difficult and not want to play with them. Problems in relating to others are often a consequence of being impulsive and hyperactive.

Problems in self-esteem

As there are difficulties in paying attention and staying on task the child with ADHD will often fall behind their peers academically. Problems with attention, hyperactivity and impulsiveness will often mean that these children are in trouble with the teacher. This along with difficulties in relating to other children can lead to poor self-esteem and behavioural problems (*Special Children* 2000b; APA 1995).

How to deal with these problems

Medication

Though this remains a controversial and emotional issue, ADHD treated with Ritalin (methylphenidate) can have very beneficial results. Psychostimulants such as Ritalin have been found to improve attention span and impulse control and decrease incidences of hyperactivity in 70–90 per cent of children with ADHD (Barkley 1998) It is important to note that Ritalin is a short-acting medication and multiple dosages need to be given. Ritalin starts to work in about twenty to forty minutes with maximum effectiveness occurring after an hour and a half. Ritalin starts to wear off after four hours. If the dosage is not correct then a condition called rebound hyperactivity could occur. What this means is that when the Ritalin starts to wear off the student becomes even more hyperactive than they ever were before taking the Ritalin. If a teacher or teaching assistant notices this then the student's doctor needs to be informed and the dosage corrected.

A specially designed environment: the ADHD classroom

Students with ADHD benefit from a highly structured environment and clear boundaries. Such children will find it difficult to cope in an open classroom where there are lots of distractions. Detweiler *et al.* (1995) see an ideal classroom as having the following characteristics:

- A small classroom with one teacher, one teaching assistant and ten children.
- A room with four walls, windows above the eye level of students (so the students can't look out) and absolutely no open space leading to other classrooms.
- A set routine with no changing of teaching and ensuring that subjects are taught in the same order every day.
- Daily programmes and weekly programme on each student's desk.
- Separate study booths for individual work. Earphones can be used to block out background noise.

Case study 4.4

Tina worked as a teaching assistant in a mainstream secondary school. One of the students Tina supported was Leon, a Year 7 student. Tina describes the following lesson with Leon. 'It was Design and Technology. The class were working on designing juggling balls. I had worked hard with Leon in coming up with a design for the juggling balls. In this class the students were to start work assembling their project. Each student had a sewing machine to work with. As well as working with and supporting Leon, I also had to deal with other students' requests to help them set up their sewing machines. I tried to get Leon started and then I went over to another student. Well, Leon was all over the place. When I was with someone else he was over at the other end of the room. Leon is incredibly agile and at one point he vaulted over an empty desk. Leon is incredibly good at gymnastics, but unfortunately in the process he knocked over the teacher's box of extra spools of thread. It took me five minutes to pick them all up and of course the teacher was not impressed with Leon. Leon was supposed to be helping me, but instead he was talking to a group of boys. In fact he had his arms around a boy's neck. Leon said he was just messing about but the other boy didn't look too happy. The lesson went very quickly and Leon unfortunately did not accomplish much.'

Obviously Leon is hard to keep on task. What could the teaching assistant do to make things easier?

- Perhaps Leon could be placed as near to the teacher as possible with his back to other students so he is not distracted by what others are doing.
- Perhaps the teaching assistant could have gone over with Leon at the beginning of class exactly what he was expected to achieve within the class. The tasks set would need to be achievable. Instructions would need to be clear and concise. The teaching assistant would need to check for understanding. Perhaps a written reminder of what he was supposed to do could be placed on his desk.
- The teaching assistant would need to observe Leon closely and catch him when he is on task and then offer lots of praise.
- Perhaps Leon could be placed near students who regularly got on with their work; these students could serve as good role models.

Communication disorders

There are many different types of communication disability. Communication is more than the spoken language but refers to an individual's ability to understand what is happening around them and to be able to make their thoughts and wishes understood by others. Communication is central to the learning process and obviously children who have difficulties with communication will find learning difficult. Unresolved communication difficulties can lead to frustration and behaviour problems and have a negative impact on self-esteem.

The sort of problems that might occur when supporting such pupils and what a teacher or teaching assistant might notice

No verbal language by the age of three

As well as a lack of language, there might be no indication that the child understands what is said to them; nor does the child attempt to communicate with others. Possible reasons for such behaviour are deafness or other neurological disabilities.

Delayed language development

Though the child is developing language their language at any given age will be more similar to a child who is very much younger. Often this delay is also evident in other areas such as social behaviour, motor skills and intellectual development. If all areas of development are affected then this would indicate global learning disabilities. An example of a conversation illustrating delayed language development is the following:

TEACHING ASSISTANT: What did you do on the weekend?
SARAH (aged 8): Swim! Big swim!
TEACHING ASSISTANT: Did you go swimming?
SARAH: Yeah! Big swim!

Language is qualitatively impaired

Here the key feature is not one of delay but of difference. For example suppose a child who has the ability to combine two or three words is asked to repeat the sentence 'Mommy is going to the shop.' A child displaying normal language development will say: 'Mommy going shop.' But a child whose understanding of language is qualitatively impaired might say: 'Is to going.' Clearly this child though able to repeat three words has not really understood what was meant by the sentence.

Difficulties in comprehension: echolalia

Often children who have problems in comprehension will also have a limited vocabulary. However, sometimes a child can exhibit what is called **echolalia**, which is the repeating of the language heard in others. Most children will do this at some times, but where this becomes an issue of concern is where the phrases are used without the purpose to communicate. Delayed echolalia is the repeating of phrases, hours, days or even weeks after the initial phrase was heard. This condition is common in the speech of some autistic children. For example, the following is a conversation between a teaching assistant and a six-year-old boy with autism.

TEACHING ASSISTANT: How many blocks do you have?
YOUNG BOY: My giddy aunt!
TEACHING ASSISTANT: Where are the blocks?
YOUNG BOY: My giddy aunt.

Difficulties in comprehension: hyperlexia

Hyperlexia is a condition where a child's reading skills greatly surpass comprehension skills. For example a child might read fluently the following: 'The recovery of extraterrestrial saucers is important to UFO enthusiasts' but have no idea what the sentence they have just read means. This condition is often associated with autism.

Difficulties in speaking (expressive language)

Problems in articulation. Here children will have problems in articulation of words, or just certain sounds. They know what they want to say; it just does not come out the right way. Sometimes children will replace one consonant with another, e.g. 'wee-waw' for 'see-saw'. Problems in articulation can be explained by many factors. Sometimes children will have conditions such as cerebral palsy or cleft palate that affect the motor movements in speech. It is thought that problems in hearing due to repeated ear infections can lead to some children having difficulties with articulation.

Stammering
Stammering, sometimes referred to as stuttering, describes speech that is tense, hesitant and jerky. Signs in speech may include:

• Blocks – getting so stuck on a word that no sound or only a strangled sound emerges.
• Sounds are prolonged, e.g. ssssssssssaid.
• Repetitions of part of word or certain sounds, e.g. 'Pre-pre-pre-present, Miss'.
• The use of fillers, e.g. 'er', 'you know', 'like'.
• A student who stammers might show signs of physical tension and nervousness such as grimacing, blinking hard, avoiding eye contact, coughing and blushing. Some students may go to great lengths to avoid talking. Student's difficulties with stammering can vary from moment to moment, hour to hour and day to day.
(British Stammering Association 1997; Berko Gleason 1997)

How to deal with these problems

The role of the speech therapist and audiologist

An *audiologist* assesses individual hearing ability, that is, an individual's ability to hear.

A *speech therapist* will evaluate the degree of communicative competence, that is, the extent to which the child can communicate. A speech therapist will use a test from the Derbyshire Language scheme to measure comprehension level, that is, how many words in a sentence a child understands. For example a teaching assistant might say to a child with severely limited communication the following:

TEACHING ASSISTANT: After lunch we are going to go swimming.
CHILD: (Runs and gets swimming gear.)
TEACHING ASSISTANT: No, not now. After lunch!
CHILD: (Starts to yell and throws swimming gear on ground.)

In this example the child is functioning at just a one-word level. The child is only responding to one key word in the sentence, in this case, swimming. The knowledge of how much a child understands can be used to enhance communication. If you know how many key words in a sentence a child can understand, then your language to the child will need to change to match their level of understanding. A speech therapist will offer advice in this area. A speech therapist will also work with students who have problems with articulation and suggest various strategies. Often teaching assistants will work with students using exercises that have been designed by the speech therapist.

Programmes such as Picture Exchange Communications

Picture Exchange Communication System (Bondy and Frost 1994) was developed to encourage communication in young autistic children by creating a meaningful communicative environment. A meaningful communicative environment is one where a student's attempts at communication are encouraged so that the student realises that there is a connection between what they do (their attempts to communicate) and what happens to them (how others respond). This system is now used with all individuals who have difficulties in this area of communication. In a sense this programme tries to teach those who have no communication the purpose of communication. There are a number of steps in this programme.

- The child is observed and what they like, their preferences, are recorded. For example one child may be very fond of cheese and onion crisps while another child has an obsession with chocolates.
- Once preferences are established, pictures of the preferences are made into picture cards.
- The child then is shown the preferred object, the packet of crisps, and the picture of the packet of crisps. The child, in order to receive the packet of crisps, must give the trainer the picture. To begin with the child might need much encouragement and prompting.
- Once the child has made the association between giving a picture card and receiving an object, more picture cards can be introduced.

In time children will be able to combine picture cards to form sentences. Individuals using this system will carry around a personalised book of picture cards (backed with Velcro), including a Velcro strip to which they add the picture cards to form sentences.

Case study 4.5

Judy, the teaching assistant, and Mrs Rogers, the French teacher, were discussing Antonia, a bright Year 9 student who had a problem with stammering and who had just joined the class. Judy stated that Antonia had approached her at break and seemed very anxious about talking in class. Mrs Rogers said that she was also aware of Antonia's anxiety and had contacted the speech therapist. Mrs Rogers said that the speech therapist had recommended the following:

- Need to talk to Antonia and ask her what would make it easier. For example, perhaps at least to begin with, she could answer the register by raising her hand.
- Must always maintain eye contact.
- Do not hurry her along or finish her words or sentences.
- Concentrate on what is being said not how it is being said.
- Give Antonia the option of doing oral tests in private rather than in front of the class.
- Possibly, when practising French phrases in class, allow Antonia to work in a small group and have all students say the phrases together.
- Allow Antonia to be in a group of friends or supportive students so that she can avoid those children who might tease her.
- Most of all, give her lots of praise.

(British Stammering Society 1997)

Sensory impairment

Generally there are two types of sensory impairment, visual impairment and hearing impairment.

The sort of problems that might occur when supporting pupils with visual impairment and what a teacher or teaching assistant might notice

Different students will have varying levels of visual impairment. Students with no sight will need to be taught **Braille** or **Moon**, while others with some sight will need adaptations made to the environment or work materials in order to make the best use of the sight that they do have.

Problems with recognition

Failure to recognise known individuals. In order to recognise an object or person, the brain needs to store some representation of that object or person, so you can say: 'Why, that's Fred. I haven't seen him for ages' or 'That's an unusual-looking car.' Very rarely the part of the brain that is responsible for these functions is damaged. Individuals who have difficulties with facial recognition are said to be suffering from a condition called **prosopagnosia**. Though these individuals have no problems with seeing, faces make no sense to them. Such individuals need to be taught alternative strategies for recognising people.

Problems with orientation

In order to find our way around our environment we need to have a visual memory of our environment stored in our mind. Obviously some people are better at remembering locations than others. Children who have severe problems in this regard will find that they get lost, even in familiar environments such as home and school. Additionally students will often have great difficulty in remembering where they have put things.

Difficulty in seeing parts of an image against a complex background

In this case the children will be able to see an object if it is on a plain background but would not be able to see the same object if it is placed on a patterned background.

Impaired depth perception

Children with problems in depth perception will find climbing up or down stairs or negotiating kerbs difficult, the reason being that when they see a line on the floor they will not know whether it indicates a step or not. Such children in trying to cope with such problems tend to stop if they see a line on the ground, especially if the line is of a different colour, and test carefully with their feet to see if there is a step or not. However, such children will often trip over kerbs as the kerb and the road are often in the same colour. Physiotherapy can help children with this condition.

Impaired perception of movement

Children with this condition will find it difficult to see and understand fast-moving objects. This could be objects, e.g. cars going whizzing by them, seeing what is around them if they are running, or making sense of fast-moving television programmes.

The sort of problems that might occur when supporting pupils with hearing impairment

Individuals will differ in regard to how much they can hear. Some individuals will be totally deaf, while others will have some hearing. Sounds are invisible vibrations that travel in waves. Sounds differ in both loudness and pitch (frequency). *Frequency* or *pitch* refers to the speed at which the sound waves vibrate. Low frequency or low pitch refers to slow-moving sound waves, while high frequency or high pitch refers to fast-moving sound waves. For example the sound of ocean waves is low in frequency, while the ring of a telephone is of a high frequency. Those children who have some hearing will need to be assessed to determine what sounds they can hear (Dutton 1997; National Deaf Children's Society 2001; Carter 1998).

How to deal with these problems

Braille and Moon are tactile systems of communication that are used by the visually impaired. Braille and Moon are composed of raised symbols that correspond to the letters of the alphabet. These raised symbols are used in combination to form words and sentences. Braille, based on raised dots, is a more complicated system to learn and is seen as too demanding for children who also have general learning disabilities (McLinden and Hendrickson 1996). The raised letters of the Moon system bear a resemblance to the letters of the alphabet as we know them.

Objects of reference

Objects of reference are specific objects that have a meaning assigned to them. Objects of reference are often used with children who have multiple disabilities. Ockelford (1998) gives the example of Peter, who is severely visually impaired and developmentally delayed. Ockelford (pp. 3–4) states that for Peter:

> the important thing was knowing when a given activity had finished . . . Peter was provided with a special tactile timetable, made up of a series of boxes in which different objects could be placed, each corresponding to a different activity. The boxes had lids that could be closed to indicate when something was over.

Hearing aids

Traditional hearing aids are basically amplifiers that pick up surrounding sounds and serve to make these sounds louder to the individual. **Cochlear implants** rely on sending electrical signals directly to the auditory nerve to provide a sensation of hearing.

Ways of developing communication and language with the hearing impaired

Auditory–oral approaches using hearing aids and implants aim to amplify (make the best of) residual hearing (what hearing ability exists) so that children can develop listening skills and spoken language.

Total communication is a view that sees hearing impaired children using different methods of communication. So in addition to using residual hearing, children would be encouraged to lip-read and use a sign system such as British Sign Language. British Sign Language is a visual language that uses hand-shapes, facial expressions, gestures and body language to communicate. Makaton is a simplified sign system that is used with individuals (both deaf and hearing) who have severe communication problems combined with learning disabilities.

Case study 4.6

Simon even with glasses had problems seeing notes written on the white board. Simon was in Year 6 at a mainstream junior school. The teacher ensured that all classroom work was presented to Simon on handouts. The teaching assistant, who was responsible for supporting Simon, would enlarge these handouts so that Simon could read them. Simon found reading material on a white background difficult as the glare interfered with his reading the words. It was suggested to the school that Simon should use coloured overlays to enhance the clarity of the text. As there were other students in the school who had problems with vision, the doors in every classroom were painted a different colour from the walls and the door handle was in a contrasting colour. This ensured that pupils could see the door and door handle and could easily enter and leave the classroom unaided.

Physical impairment

Physical impairments is a term that includes many conditions. Some of the more common conditions include muscular dystrophy, cystic fibrosis, spina bifida, cerebral palsy, diabetes and epilepsy.

The sort of problems that might occur when supporting such pupils and how to deal with these problems

As there are so many different types of physical impairment this section on areas of difficulty and ways forward will focus on general concerns and strategies.

Movement

Many students with physical disabilities will have restricted movement.

- The role of **physiotherapists** and **occupational therapists** involves the assessment and treatment of disorders of movement. Physiotherapists treat such disorders using methods such as exercise, manipulation and heat. An occupational therapist is interested in what daily living skills an individual has. Occupational therapists are also responsible for the assessment and provision of suitable equipment and for suggesting how to adapt the environment of home, school or work so the individual can be as independent as possible.
- A student with a condition such as cerebral palsy might have problems with movement. They might be in a wheelchair and have stiffness in their muscles. Physiotherapists will advise parents and carers how best to lift and position an individual. In terms of the educational environment they will advise on the best posture, working environment and seating for the child. If there is stiffness in the muscles the physiotherapist will suggest certain exercises and physical activity that can help promote good patterns of move-

ment. An occupational therapist would be involved in assessing what skills are missing and whether these physical and learning skills can be developed through the use of specialised equipment. Such equipment could include adapted tricycles or a gait trainer, designed to encourage walking.

Speech and language

The role of the speech therapist is to help individuals make the maximum use of their communication skills. A speech therapist will work with all individuals who have problems with their speech, understanding spoken and/or written language, using language and eating and drinking. Some children will have delayed language due to limited opportunities to play and explore. The speech therapist working with other therapists can suggest suitable learning activities. Some physical conditions, such as cerebral palsy, will affect the motor movements responsible for talking. In some cases an alternative system of communication is suggested. For individuals who have good motor control in their hands and arms, a sign language might be appropriate. For others a communication board where individuals point to letters or pictures/symbols might be more appropriate.

Encouraging a sense of independence

Regardless of disability, everyone would like to be treated with respect and dignity. Many adults with physical disabilities will say that it is society's attitudes to them that are the most difficult to deal with. This attitude can be summed up by the expression 'Would they like sugar?' Children with physical disabilities need to be helped to be as independent as possible. They need to be encouraged to make choices.

As a teaching assistant it is important to know and understand the needs of the particular student you are supporting. In many cases you will be putting into practice many of the interventions suggested by the various therapists.

Case study 4.7

Claire, age nine, attends a special school. She has cerebral palsy and no spoken communication. Owing to Claire's difficulty in controlling the movements of her arms, a sign language was not seen as appropriate.

However, Claire can point to objects. She can also shake her head to indicate yes or no and she has a beautiful smile and laugh when she is happy. At school Claire loves the multi-sensory room. **Multi-sensory rooms** offer a range of experiences involving sight, sound, touch and smell. What Claire likes best is moving the specially adapted switches that control the combinations of light and sound. Claire's teacher states that this helps Claire feel that she has control over her environment. When Claire started at the school careful thought was given as to how the school could offer Claire meaningful choices. It was decided that when Claire was involved in any activity she would be given a choice between two activities. When she is involved in a literacy session she would be given a choice between listening to the story on tape or having someone read to her. When Claire is in the swimming pool, she is given a choice about what colour flotation device she holds on to. As the teacher said, 'It is through constantly having choices about all aspects of her life that we can best encourage a sense of independence.'

Bilingual/multilingual pupils

The first point to make about working with bilingual/multilingual pupils is to know the language background of the child. Some children might come from a background where they have an understanding of two languages, e.g. they talk to mother in Spanish and talk to Dad in English. On the other hand a child could come from a family that has recently immigrated, or has received refugee status and understand no, or very little English. To recap what was said in Chapter 2, a child beginning school with no English will usually take two years to develop basic interpersonal communication skills and five to seven years to achieve cognitive academic language proficiency, the standard necessary to cope with GCSEs.

Hester (Barrs *et al.* 1988) outlined four stages of language development as: (1) new to English, (2) becoming familiar with English, (3) becoming confident as a user of English, (4) a very fluent user of English in most social and learning contexts. Students who have already learned to read and write in their first language will show the following behaviours at the above stages of second language development (Hall 1995, p. 36):

Stage 1 New to English

- Student will listen and respond mainly in first language.
- Student is often silent in class. Uses second language to say single words and simple phrases.
- Can read simple words. Student relies on pictures for clues to meaning.
- Begins to spell single words and begins to spell phonetically.

Stage 2 Becoming familiar with English

- Student will need to have all instructions repeated. However, the student can understand some of what is being said in class and can follow simple instructions and explanations.
- Student now participates in informal discussions and begins to participate in group work.
- Student begins to understand some of the material that is read and becomes able to discuss what has been read.
- Student can now write short passages. Begins to use punctuation and begins to understand language rules such as present and future tense.

Stage 3 Becoming confident as a language user

- Student now understands a great deal of what is being said and can follow complex instructions.
- Student becomes more confident in speaking. At this point spoken language still exceeds reading and spelling ability.
- Student is able to read and understand more complex texts.
- Writing skills have improved but student will still make mistakes in regard to difficult vocabulary and complex grammatical constructions.

Stage 4 Fluent

- Student is now fluent in regards to listening and speaking in the second language.
- Student is a capable and confident reader and can now skim read.
- Student can confidently write in a number of different styles.

The sort of problems that might occur when supporting such pupils and possible explanations for such problems

The child is exceptionally quiet in class

- This could be part of the normal stage of second language acquisition.
- However, if a child starts school and is delayed in their first language then an assessment of their first language abilities needs to be carried out to determine the extent of the delay. This is necessary to establish whether there are any additional special needs.

The child is not progressing

- An assessment for special needs, such as dyslexia, needs to be carried out.
- The work set might be too difficult. A teacher might wrongly assume on the basis of the student's confidence in informal conversations that they understand more than they do. An ability to communicate on an informal level does not necessarily mean that the student will understand abstract academic language.
- A child might not be learning due to environmental stress. This stress could result from bullying and racism. If the child is from a refugee family there could be, depending on family circumstances, financial stress and painful emotional memories stemming from their life in their country of origin.

(Hall 1995)

How to deal with these problems

There are a number of suggestions:

- In the early stages of language development it is suggested that the first language be used within the classroom to support learning. It is recommended that a bilingual assistant support the child for at least some of the time.
- If there is a group of students who share the same first language, it is felt that it would not be a good idea to put them all in one group. It would be better to have mixed groups of children, a few children who are beginning to learn English with the majority of children who are fluent in English. In this case the fluent speakers can

help and serve as role models for the children who are beginning to learn English.

- It is important for children who are trying to learn a second language to be seated with students who will support and help them.
- The use of bilingual or translated texts.
- The work set will need to be differentiated. Differentiation has been defined as adapting work to the differing capabilities of students with the aim of supporting learning. The work needs to be geared to their understanding but at the same time be suitably age-appropriate, cognitively/intellectually demanding and motivating.

Reflective component

Case study 4.8

Mary works in a mainstream school supporting the Year 6 class. One of the students Mary supports is Alison. Alison has both Asperger's and dyslexia.

Description of event (What happened? What should have happened?)

The teacher had assigned the class an essay to write and I was sitting with Alison working through an essay plan. Alison also prefers to write her rough work in pencil. However, her pencils always have to be sharpened up to a certain level for her to write. When Alison is somewhat anxious about work she tends to press too hard on her pencil, which means she has to get up and go the back of the class to get her favourite sharpener. I have suggested that we have the sharpener on her desk but Alison is firm that the pencil sharpener is kept at the back of the class. Well, off Alison went to get the sharpener but on her way back I noticed that Alison hit every student she passed with the pencil sharpener. The pencil sharpener was very light and most students just smiled and said: 'Oh, it's you Alison,' but I could tell that a few of the students were fed up. Anyway it was then time to go out for break, but I noticed that Alison was all by herself and not for the first time that week. I know the incident with the pencil sharpener was really a minor thing but I thought I had better mention it to the teacher. The teacher was very interested in my observation and stated that she too had noticed that Alison was finding it more and more difficult to get along with the students in the class. The teacher said she would mention it to the Senco and later in the day she came back to me and said that the Senco would be soon working with Alison on a social story and that we would discuss it later.

Feelings (What did I feel? What did the students feel?)

I think I was right to tell the teacher about the pencil sharpener incident. What did Alison think? Well, with Alison it is difficult to know. I think she misses the other girls talking with her at break, but I don't think she realises how she annoys them sometimes.

Evaluation (What was good? What was difficult?)

Well, we accomplished a fair bit with the essay plan, even though Alison wasted considerable time with having to sharpen her pencil.

Self-assessment

Your task is to complete the reflective log. Remember to use the headings: *Analysis* (How do I make sense of this? Why did it happen? When writing this use what you now know about ASD to explain Alison's behaviour), *In conclusion* (What else could I have done?), *Action plan* (Next time I would . . .).

Chapter 5

Preventing and managing emotional/behavioural difficulties

Defining emotional and behavioural problems

Those working in schools can tell stories of students who exhibit difficult behaviour. But what is difficult behaviour? Difficult behaviour could include those students who constantly arrive late for class, shout and swear, destroy school property, disrupt classes to such an extent that other students are prevented from learning and in some cases threaten and attack other students and staff. Difficult or problematic behaviour could also include students who are extremely quiet and withdrawn. Student behaviour is an important issue, as teachers cannot teach if they cannot create an environment where it is possible for all students to learn. It is the role of teaching assistants to aid the teachers in creating such an environment. Today this challenging or disruptive behaviour is referred to as **emotional behavioural difficulties**, or EBD for short. In stressing the impact that EBD has on those working in a school EBD has been defined as:

> Behaviour which is manifested verbally or physically and which covertly challenges to varying degrees and in a variety of ways – the authority of the teacher or the school. This can include a catalogue of comparatively minor misdemeanours which, whilst not immediately challenging the authority of teachers demand the expenditure of inordinate amounts of teacher time and energy.
>
> (Charlton and David 1993)

Unacceptable and problematic behaviour can be classified according to severity, with level 1 being the least problematic and level 3 outlining behaviour of a very serious nature (Daniels *et al.* 1999, pp. 145–6, 164).

Level 1

- Disrupting other children. Chatting in class. Not on task. Out of seat. Wandering about the class. Fidgeting in seat.
- Forgets to bring in needed equipment or materials. Arrives late. Careless damage to property.
- Answers back. Makes inappropriate noises. Minor bad language.
- Difficulty in getting on with other students in the class. Difficulty in sharing and co-operating with others. Tells lies with the intention of getting others in trouble. Sometimes emotional. Minor problems in self-esteem.

Level 2

- More of level 1 behaviour.
- Deliberate defiance. Refusal to do work or follow instructions.
- Threatening behaviour to other students and teachers. Incidents of bullying. Isolated acts of violence, e.g. hitting, kicking, punching, etc.
- Easily reduced to tears. Easily reduced to outbursts of anger/ tantrums. Withdrawn. Isolated from peer group. Problems with self-esteem. Cannot express feelings.
- Minor vandalism and stealing.

Level 3

- More of level 2 behaviour.
- Persistent episodes of defiance, abusive language and bullying.
- Creates major disruptions in class on a regular basis.
- Frequent episodes of aggressive behaviour causing deliberate injury.
- Serious acts of vandalism to school buildings and property.
- Often leaves school premises without consent.

The above levels of behaviour are not definitive, that is, they do not include all examples of behaviours that are displayed by students with emotional or behavioural difficulties. Further this list would need to be adapted to reflect the age of the students. Being emotional is to be expected from a reception student. However, if a Year 10 student constantly bursts into tears then you would be right in being concerned. It is also important to note that students with EBD will not display all of these behaviours. However, the above way of categorising unacceptable and problematic behaviour does give an insight into what those working in the schools experience and shows how these behaviours can vary in severity.

Aspects of culture, upbringing, home circumstances and physical and emotional health that could influence the pupil's interactions with others

There are many outside influences that could explain or account for a student's behaviour. Possibly the student has learned to behave in such a disruptive way. The behaviourists (Chapter 1) state that there is always a reason for any behaviour. This viewpoint would argue that if a student continually behaves in a challenging or disturbing manner then it is because they have in the past been rewarded for this type of behaviour. Possible rewards are attention. Any attention, even negative attention, that is, a teacher screaming and yelling at them, is better than no attention. Students might get attention and respect from their peers for acting up. Possibly being thrown out of a class is preferable to being in a class where they have no idea of how to do the work. In this sense acting up and being sent out prevents others students from finding out that they can't actually do the work. If a student can't succeed academically perhaps they can succeed at being a failure.

Bandura (Chapter 1), in his social learning theory, would argue that students learn disruptive and challenging behaviour by observing and imitating others. Students can learn inappropriate behaviour by watching what happens to other students who behave in such a way at school. Students might observe and learn disruptive behaviour in their home environment, in the playground or out in the streets with their friends.

Harris (1997) in outlining her **group socialisation theory** argues that it is the group that an individual belongs to that determines their behaviour. For a student this group would be their peer group. A student would learn rules about what is appropriate behaviour from the peer group. A problem often occurs when the peer group, culture or sub-culture that the student identifies with is in conflict with the culture of the school. For example the culture of the school would promote values and attitudes such as respect for other pupils and staff, commitment to learning, pursuit of academic, social and athletic excellence, wearing the school uniform with pride, etc. However, not all peer groups and sub-cultures would see these attitudes as desirable and there lies the problem. For some students handing in homework, being seen to work in class and doing what they are told would not be seen as being 'cool'.

Another aspect that influences the student's interactions with others is *mental health*. Mental health is defined as:

> maintaining a good level of personal and social functioning. For children and young people, this means getting on with others, both peers and adults participating in educative and other social activities and having a positive self-esteem. Mental health is about coping and adjusting to the demands of growing up.
>
> (DfEE 2001, p. iv)

While this definition stresses what children should be working towards, problems with mental health in children and young adults could include:

- Eating disorders: anorexia nervosa, bulimia nervosa.
- Emotional disorders: excessive fears, anxiety, depression.
- Conduct disorders: stealing, fire setting, torturing animals, aggression.
- Attachment disorders: 'Children who are markedly distressed or socially impaired as a result of an extremely abnormal pattern of attachment to parents or major care-givers'.

> (DfEE 2001, p. 1)

From the point of view of those working in a school, a child with mental health issues will often be seen as having emotional and behavioural difficulties. In discussing mental health much research has gone into identifying risk and resilience factors. **Risk factors** suggest that there are situations that can make a child more susceptible or more likely to have mental health problems. **Resilience factors** on the other hand identify those factors that serve to protect the child from mental health problems.

Risk factors include:

- Child has/had insecure relationships with parents/caregivers, low self-esteem, specific learning disabilities, experienced academic failure.
- Family is characterised by hostile relationships and open conflict. The family unit has experienced breakdown and is unable to provide clear and consistent discipline. The family unit might be coping with issues such as death, bereavement, mental illness in a family member or a family member in prison. In severe cases the child might experience physical, emotional or sexual abuse within the family. In general the family is unable to meet the needs of the child.
- The environment in which the child lives is disadvantaged. There is a high level of poverty, homelessness and limited social opportunities.

Resilience factors include:

- Child has/had secure relationships with parents/caregivers, an average or above average level of intelligence, good social and communication skills, willingness to seek and accept help and advice, a sense of humour and a religious faith.
- At least one parent provides affection, love, emotional support, and clear and consistent discipline, and encourages the child in educational achievement.
- The environment in which the child lives has many advantages. There are good housing, high employment rates, a high standard of living, good community relationships and many affordable social opportunities.

(DfEE 2001, pp. 4–6)

On a further note we could talk about the impact that physical health can have on a child's interactions with others. There are several issues here. One issue is communication. A condition such as cerebral palsy might effect the person's ability to communicate. A difficulty in communication which is not resolved by speech therapy, or teaching the student alternative ways of communicating, can lead to frustration, which in turn can lead to aggression or acting up. In some cases a student could be suffering from a progressive illness, whereby they gradually lose skills and abilities. In these situations the student and those close to the student will need considerable emotional support.

Table 5.1 Intervention strategies a teaching assistant might use

Intervention strategies	Example of teaching assistant intervention
Reminder of rules and codes of behaviour. This can be given to groups or on an individual basis. It can be given before an activity or during an activity to remind the group how they should be behaving	The following strategy is used with a reception class. 'Now, Orange Group, before we start we need to remind ourselves of our listening rules. In order to listen we need to put on our thinking heads.' (Teaching assistant points to head). 'We need to listen with our ears' (points to ears). 'We need to listen with our eyes' (points to eyes). 'We need to listen with our mouth' (points to mouth). 'And we need to listen with our hands' (points to hands). 'Shall we repeat that? Now if anyone forgets, I will point to the rule on the board'
The look	When I am supporting the teacher during the literacy hour I sit at the front facing the children. If I see one of the children doing something they shouldn't be, I try to get their attention and then I give them a look and mouth the word 'Behave.' This often works
Moving closer to students. Separating disruptive students	I work in a secondary school. When I am in class, and I realise there is a disturbance in some part of the room, I will go over to the students and casually ask how things are going. Sometimes this is enough to get them back on task. When I work with groups sometimes there are two students who just cannot get on or sometimes they are getting on too well and they are not doing their work. If that is the case I get the students to change places. If this doesn't work and one student is disrupting the others and preventing them from working I ask the teacher if I can move the disruptive student to somewhere quieter
Private chat with student	I work in a secondary school. My job is to support several students who have statements. One day Jason who I was supporting was getting very wound up by another student. It was not that this student was saying anything to Jason but I knew that Jason and him did not get on. I asked the teacher if I could have a quiet chat with Jason in the hall for a few minutes. I reminded Jason of his behavioural targets and how well he had been doing and I asked him if he could remember what he should do when he felt bothered by another student. He said that he should try to ignore it.

After that we went back in the class and Jason worked very well. I felt I needed to take him outside as what I wanted to say to him was better said in confidence

Giving choices and warning of consequences

Whenever a student is misbehaving, I will remind them of what they should be doing. If they don't do what they should be doing I give them another chance. I say to them, 'You have a choice. You can do what I say and get on with your work or I will have to inform the teacher of your behaviour.' If they still don't do what they should I inform the teacher. It is important that students know there are consequences for their actions

Removing the audience

I work in a junior school. I was working in a group. The group was working on a worksheet on fractions. John told the group in a loud voice that he wasn't going to work and that he was going to go on strike and that school was useless. I moved John to a separate table. I removed the audience as I felt that most of what he said was said to impress the others. I asked him what was the matter. At first he didn't say anything, but then he finally admitted he had forgotten how to do fractions

Using humour. Boosting self-esteem

Amy was very disappointed by her drawing of an elephant. She said she was going to rip it up. I then quickly got a piece of paper and drew an elephant. I said to her, 'Well, just look at my attempt. It looks more like my Aunt Ethel.' Amy laughed and felt much better about her picture

Encouraging empathy and respect

Whenever a student swears at me, I ask them if I ever swear at them. They say no. I then ask how they like it when someone swears at them. I then say, 'Well I expect you to treat me with the same respect that I treat you'

Asking student to behave in a manner that expects the student to respond

For example, 'Joe, we have a rule about sharing play equipment at break. I expect you to give others a turn on the bike. Thank you'

Positive strategies/ rewarding appropriate good behaviour, praise, stickers, merit points

After Jason, who has a history of winding other students up and starting fights, worked quietly all lesson and completed his worksheet, I said how good his work was and how proud I was of his behaviour

Intervention strategies appropriate for pupils with behavioural and emotional difficulties

As challenging and problematic behaviour exists on many levels, so do intervention strategies. Most teaching assistants will be directly involved at the lower levels of intervention. Table 5.1 outlines strategies that teaching assistants might use. The examples show what teaching assistants can do on a day-to-day level to help the teacher create an environment where it is possible for all students to learn. Obviously there will be situations of a more serious nature where the role of a teaching assistant is to inform a teacher of what is happening. Schools will have codes of behaviour and established ways of dealing with very disruptive behaviour. Schools will use sanctions such as detentions, loss of privileges, or requiring students to stay in at break. At a secondary level the school might operate an 'on call system', where if a teacher is in difficulty, they ask a co-operative student to take a card to the office. This will signal that the teacher needs assistance. A senior member of staff will then come to the class and remove the disruptive student from the class. In the event of very serious episodes of challenging behaviour the parents of the student will be brought in and in some cases students will be excluded from the school. If a student is having difficulties of an emotional nature, for example, with depression or anxiety the school will refer the student to counsellors or pastoral support.

The importance of recognising and rewarding positive behaviour

We have talked previously about the many reasons why a student displays disruptive behaviour. Though reprimands are used on students, the most effective way of dealing with disruptive behaviour is to reward appropriate and good behaviour, that is, 'Catch them while they are being good.' If you notice a child doing something good, tell them immediately. In order for the reward to be effective, the student must know what behaviour they are being rewarded for. Rewards motivate the student to repeat the good behaviour and serve to boost the student's self-esteem.

Negotiation skills: giving choices and consequences

Students need to be helped to see that they are in part responsible for what happens to them. For example:

STUDENT: Mr Todd gave me a detention.
TEACHING ASSISTANT: What did you do?
STUDENT: I didn't do anything. Mr Todd is always picking on me.

Students need to be made aware that their behaviour has an effect on others. Students need to be told how their behaviour makes other people feel. At this point the teaching assistant may ask for more details.

TEACHING ASSISTANT: Tell me exactly what happened.
STUDENT: Mr Todd said I was bullying Ted. I wasn't bullying. I did have my arm round his neck but I was just mucking about.

Of course at this point the teaching assistant is not surprised that the student got a detention. However, in order to improve the student's behaviour, the student first needs to be aware of why he/she received a detention. Students need to be aware that they have choices in how they behave and that every choice has a consequence. Students need to be aware that they can make good choices or bad choices.

Following this example the teaching assistant might say:

TEACHING ASSISTANT: If you put your arm round someone else's neck they might think that you are trying to strangle them. If a teacher sees you doing it they will think the same and you will be accused of bullying. If you bully someone then the consequence is that you will be in trouble and that you will have a detention. If you mind your own business and get on with work you won't get a detention. The choice is up to you.

This strategy can be used to both reflect on why a student got into trouble and as a means of preventing future incidents.

Monitoring the group to spot signs of conflict at an early stage

It is obviously better to prevent a major incident than to have to deal with it. But to prevent an incident you need to be sensitive to the cues, both verbal and non-verbal, that indicate that the student is 'building up' to an episode of challenging behaviour. However, different students will react differently. Here observation and knowledge of the students you are working with are crucial.

Non-verbal signs to look out for (Hewett 2000):

- Students being restless, out of seat, pacing the class, or becoming very still and quiet.
- Increased eye contact, eyes widening or reluctance to make eye contact.
- Facial tension. Threatening gestures, clenched fists. Trembling all over. Attempts at self-control, e.g. clasping hands. Face going red or white.
- Invasion of personal space, e.g. 'in your face'.
- Inconsistent and unusual behaviour.

Verbal signs to look out for:

- Muttering phrases (e.g. 'No one ever f****** listens. You're all the same'). Making threats ('I'm going to get you').
- Performing in front of an audience, trying to get audience on their side.
- Voice become louder and higher in pitch. Inappropriate laughter.

De-escalation strategies, or ways to make the potentially dangerous situation less dangerous

- If there are others students in the room and they are in potential danger then the students should be removed for their safety. This also eliminates the audience, which may help defuse the situation.
- If you know what has triggered the outburst, sometimes removing the trigger can defuse the situation.
- Allow space between you and the aggressor. If possible make sure the student has an escape route. In extreme cases think about how you would get out of the situation and pieces of school equipment that could be used as a weapon against you.
- Keep normal eye contact. Try to appear calm and non-confrontational. Do not stand too close. Do not stand 'square-on', but rather at an angle. Don't make matters worse by losing your temper. Talk softly. Try to get the student to calm down. Wait for assistance.
- Sometimes it is helpful to try to distract the student by focusing the student on something completely different.

- Sometimes all you can do is stand back, do nothing and wait until the person has calmed down.

(Hewett 2000)

Recovery strategies

Let's take for example a situation where a Year 9 student blows up in class, throws several chairs around and in the process breaks a window. At that moment it seems that the worst is over and that the student is calming down. At this point the student is said to be in the recovery phase. At this point, teaching staff need to avoid doing things that could make the student engage in further acts of aggression. No matter what the student has done, what they need at this stage is reassurance and compassion. The advice is to avoid blaming the student and to act positively towards the student. Students at some point will need to talk about their behaviour; however, they will differ in terms of when they will be ready to talk. Of course it is difficult to be calm and reassuring to someone who has acted in a totally inappropriate manner. Counsellors often talk about how you can condemn the behaviour but still value the person (Hewett 2000).

Reflective component

Case study 5.1: primary school

Jane works as a teaching assistant in a Year 2 class. Jane wrote:

Description of event (What happened? What should have happened?)

I was working with a small group of students on number skills. They were all working on worksheets. We had one eraser at the table and one child, Sarah, had taken rather a shine to it, and insisted that it was hers and would not share it with the other children. I asked Sarah to share the eraser, but she refused. She said that the other students could go and use one from the other table. I again asked Sarah to share and she said: 'You can't make me.' I told her I had no choice but to go and tell the teacher. I told the teacher and she stopped and said to the class what did they think of a student who was rude and wouldn't share? The teacher said that this was just not acceptable behaviour. At this point Sarah burst into tears and said,

'I am so sorry.' Sarah was very upset and it took her fifteen minutes to calm down.

Feelings (How did I feel? How do I think the students feel?)

I felt that I was right to tell the teacher but I was shocked by how upset Sarah was. I kept thinking that maybe there was something I could have done to encourage Sarah to share.

Evaluation (What was good? What was difficult?)

Analysis (How do I make sense of this?)

In conclusion (What else could I have done?)

Action plan (What will I do next time?)

Self-assessment

Your task is to complete the reflective log. (Hint: consider some of the strategies we have talked about.)

Case study 5.2: secondary school

Sandra reports:

Description of event (What happened?)

Well, Jeff is never an easy student to work with. He is always late for class, he never brings the right equipment. It is very difficult to get Jeff motivated. Today Jeff had decided to sit beside Wayne. Those two always wind each other up. The teacher will usually separate them but today we had a supply teacher. I have several other students who I support in this class and I started to get them settled first. Then there was an almighty commotion and I looked up to see Jeff throwing Wayne's books out of the first-floor window. Wayne was jumping up and down and looked as if he was about to throw a punch. I immediately went over to the boys and as I knew both of them very well I said that I was ashamed of their behaviour. This seemed to take the steam out of them. At this point on call had arrived and Jeff was taken out of the class. Wayne was very upset about his books. Then Sam piped up that it didn't matter as Wayne couldn't read anyway. Now it looked like Wayne was going to take a punch at Sam. I asked the supply teacher if I could take Wayne out of the class for a moment as he looked very steamed up. At that point Wayne said: 'I'm going to f★★★★★★ kill Sam.' I said to him in the hall that I knew that he was very upset about his books but getting angry at Sam would not make it any better and that Sam was well out of line to have made that remark. I said he had a choice: he could either get angry at Sam and face the consequences of being taken to the Head of Year or he could go with me and collect his books and get back to work. I could see that Wayne was thinking about this, but in the end he went with me and we got his books, he went back to class and I made sure he was sitting away from Sam. Wayne worked hard for the rest of the session and after the session I told him that I was very proud that he had made the right choice and gave him a commendation.

Self-assessment

Your task is to imagine that you are Sandra and complete the reflective log. Remember to use the headings.

Chapter 6

Establishing effective working relationships with pupils and colleagues

Basic principles of effective communication with pupils

The role of teaching assistants is to work with the teacher in order to support the learning of pupils. Now, to support learning a teaching assistant must communicate effectively with pupils. Effective communication is said to happen when there is open and honest communication, when dialogue is handled in a constructive manner and when there is consistent and effective support. These are the principles of effective communication. But maybe a little more needs to be said about what these principles actually mean in practice.

- *Open and honest communication.* The pupil should feel able to say what they are truly feeling. However, this requires that the pupil trust the teaching assistant. In turn the teaching assistant should be open and honest with the pupil. This sounds great, but how do you say those things that are difficult to say, e.g. 'If you weren't so bone lazy, I am sure you could do your work,' and on the other hand how do you respond when a pupil says 'I hate you'? This brings us on to the second principle.
- *Ability to handle dialogue in a constructive manner.* So it seems that though we should aim for open and honest communication, the way we talk to or respond to a student should be conducted in a manner that is positive, sensitive to the feelings of others and that does not undermine a pupil's self-esteem. Again it is important to use constructive feedback (see p. 48). Communication that follows the above principles will serve as an example to the students of how adults should talk to each other.

- *Consistent and effective support.* This principle states that this method of constructive and honest communication needs to be consistent. That is, we should try to act in this way, to all pupils, at all times.

The next sections on active listening and interpreting body language give suggestions and handy tips on how we can effectively communicate with pupils.

Techniques of active listening

As individuals we have conversations all the time and listening to what others say is an important part of a conversation. However, there is a difference between **active listening** and social listening, which we do on an everyday basis. Active listening involves communicating, or showing to the person we are talking to, that we have heard what they have said and that we understand what they are saying. Sometimes this type of listening is referred to as rewarding listening. The following outlines a ten-skill approach to rewarding listening (Nelson-Jones 1993, pp. 87–108).

1 *Know the difference between me and you.* This step involves trying to get inside a student's mind in order to understand the world from their perspective. In order to do this you need to realise that as you have a view of yourself and of the student, they have their own unique view of themselves and you. For example you might see yourself as patiently trying to encourage an uncooperative and lazy student to work while they feel that you are a nagging, unreasonable teaching assistant who is trying to get them to do an impossible task.

2 *Possess an attitude of respect and acceptance.* Here we need to accept that a student has their own unique thoughts and feelings. We need to listen to what a student says with respect and without making judgements. Here it is important to separate our emotions from the students' emotions. We all bring our own emotional selves to work. For example we might have had an argument with our partner or our children, the car might have broken down on the way to work, the central heating might have packed in, but whatever we are feeling it is important that we don't let our own emotional state influence how we respond to the students.

3   *Send good body messages.* We can communicate that we are listening by using positive body language. Positive body language would involve having a relaxed posture, facing the student, leaning slightly forward, maintaining eye contact and using appropriate facial expressions. When talking to a young child we might get down to their level. It is also important to respect a student's personal space as getting physically too close may be seen as threatening.

4   *Send good voice messages.* It is important that we are aware of aspects of our voice. *Volume* refers to how quietly or loudly we are talking. Obviously a very loud voice can overwhelm or frighten, while a very quiet voice could lead the student to think the teaching assistant was weak. *Pitch* implies how high or low our voice sounds. A very high-pitched voice might indicate anxiety. *Articulation* refers to how clearly we are speaking. Obviously it is important that what we say is clearly heard by the student. *Emphasis* refers to how expressive our voice is. Too much emphasis on words and we might come across as a would-be actor, while too little emphasis could come across as being cold. However, the right amount of emphasis can reflect emotion back to the student.

5   *Use openers, small rewards and open-ended questions.* Openers give students permission to talk and tell them you are prepared to listen. For example you might ask, 'You seem upset. Are you all right?' Small rewards are brief verbal and non-verbal responses that you give to the students that tell them that you are listening and are interested in what they have to say. Examples of small rewards are nods, raised eyebrows, good eye contact and soothing voice sounds such as 'uh-hmm'. Open-ended questions encourage the student to keep talking. (For a further discussion on questions see pp. 52–5.)

6   *Reword.* Rewording involves listening to the content of what the student has said and rewording or rephrasing what they have said back to them. This strategy has many advantages. It clarifies what the student has said. It shows them that you are listening and perhaps it helps the student understand what they are trying to say. For example:

STUDENT: I can't do it . . . I just can't do it.
TEACHING ASSISTANT: You can't do your homework.

7   *Reflect feelings.* Reflecting feelings involves not only listening to what the student says but also observing *how* the student says what they do. In particular you are looking for a mis-match between what they say and how they say it. For example a student may say they are fine, but there might be tears in their eyes. In this case you might say to the student (that is, reflect feelings back to the student by saying): 'You say you are fine, but there are tears in your eyes. Perhaps you are trying to be brave?'

8   *Reflect feelings and reasons.* This involves reflecting back to the student their feelings but also the reason for their feelings. This strategy can show to the student that you do understand them. For example:

> STUDENT: She's so unfair. Sam didn't do his homework and he didn't get a detention.
> TEACHING ASSISTANT: You're angry with the teacher as she gave you a detention but not Sam?

9   *Avoid unrewarding 'don'ts'.* This step advises the listener to avoid the following pitfalls. The advice is:

(a) Don't take control of the conversation.
(b) Don't judge or moralise.
(c) Don't dismiss the student's emotions or worries by simply reassuring them that it will turn out all right.
(d) Don't assign blame, e.g. 'Well, it's all your own fault.'
(e) Don't fake attention.
(f) Don't put time restrictions on the conversation, e.g. 'Well, I only have five minutes, so we better make this quick.'

10   *Avoid poor thinking skills.* To be an effective listener you need to think about how you respond to a student bearing in mind all the above points.

Obviously active listening is a skill. While these strategies are designed to help you communicate with students, there will be times when from what the student says it is obvious that the student will need someone who is professionally skilled to talk to. Perhaps a few examples of how a teaching assistant could use these strategies would be helpful at this point.

Case study 6.1

I work supporting Dave in a number of classes. Dave had not handed in homework since the term began and now he was being given a detention for every piece of homework missed. I just happened to bump into Dave as the final bell had gone and asked him where he was going. Dave said briefly that he had a detention to go to for not handing in his history homework. I asked him if he had any problems with his homework that prevented him from handing in his homework. Dave said no, but wouldn't look me in the eye and seemed very uncomfortable. I suggested that perhaps rather than going to the detention he would rather go with me to the learning support unit where we could talk in private about his homework. Dave looked pleased and said yes. I told him to go to the learning support unit while I check with his history teacher if this would be all right. The history teacher did think that it was a good idea, so I went back to the learning support unit to talk with Dave. Dave seemed pleased to see me and relieved that he did not have to go to the detention. I asked him if he was all right as he seemed a bit fed up. Dave mumbled that he was fed up with spending every day in detention. I told him that I would be fed up if I was him. I asked Dave again why he didn't do his homework and if there was some sort of problem. He said no, but looked very upset and again would not look me in the eye. I leaned forward, caught his eye and said that I was concerned that by not doing his homework he was getting into lots of trouble and that there must be some reason. Dave looked up and said tearfully that 'it was too hard'. I said, 'So you are not doing your homework because you are finding it too difficult?' Dave said that he didn't understand what the teacher wanted him to do, and even when he did know he didn't know how to begin. I said, 'It must be very difficult to do homework if you don't know what to do and where to begin,' and then I asked Dave if there was anyone at home to help him. Dave said that Mom used to help, but that Nanny had just had a stroke and had moved in with them and that now, when he went home, he was expected to help with the younger children. I told Dave that in the classes that I was in with him we would go through the homework together and that, with his permission, I would talk to his teachers. I then suggested that instead of going to detention every day that he should join the school's homework club and that they would help him complete his work. When Dave left the unit he was much happier.

Interpreting non-verbal communication

As the above case study shows, we not only communicate with words, but we also communicate through eye contact, tone of voice and body movements. To communicate effectively we need to be aware of both our own and others' methods of **non-verbal communication** (Table 6.1). Non-verbal communication (NVC) is important for several reasons:

- We use NVC to add emphasis to what we are saying.
- We use NVC as a form of feedback, to tell others what we are thinking and feeling.
- NVC tells us a lot about a person's attitude.
- We need to be aware of our non-verbal communication as much of it is done very quickly and without thought.
- When there is a conflict between what a person says and the manner, in which it is said, people will attach more significance to how it is said. In this case non-verbal communication is seen as a better indicator of what a person is truly thinking and feeling.

(Hayes 1984)

Basic principles of working with groups

Stages in the development of groups

Tuckman and Jensen (1977) outlined five stages of group development. These are as follows:

- *Forming.* At this stage the group has just met or has been just put together. At this point in time they are not properly a group but a collection of individuals. At this stage the group begins to get to know each other and begins to set ground rules for ways of working.
- *Storming.* At this stage a group may experience conflict as they try to work out ways of working together. There could be arguments regarding what is done, how it is done and who does what. For example students might argue about who is in charge.
- *Norming.* Here the group decides/agrees on ways of working. Once this has been established then they can get on with the task of working together.

Table 6.1 Non-verbal communication

Type	Interpreting signals	How to demonstrate value and interest through body language
Posture	Sitting or standing upright and looking directly at the other person indicates that we are interested in what that other person has to say Slouching, facing another direction and not maintaining eye contact indicates that we are bored or just not interested in what the other person has to say	Maintain an upright body posture and maintain eye contact
Eye contact	Generally maintaining eye contact indicates interest in the other person Gazing around the room indicates that we are not interested in the other person or what the other person is saying Analysis of conversations indicates that we maintain eye contact with the other person when we start a conversation. Afterwards we might gaze away but re-engage eye contact when we want to emphasise a point or to indicate that we have stopped talking and now it is their turn to speak	Use eye contact to indicate interest, to emphasise a point and as a cue to the other person that it is their turn to talk

Gestures, body movements and facial expressions	Gestures such as nods, small sounds indicate your approval and that you are listening	Make use of gestures, such as nods and small sounds that indicate approval.
	From a very early age children can recognise and understand the meanings behind facial expressions. There are believed to be seven main types of facial expression. These are happiness, surprise, fear, anger, sadness, disgust and interest	Mirror facial expressions. Use appropriate facial expressions
	When we are listening to someone we tend to mirror their facial expressions. Thus if the speaker seems upset and worried we tend to adopt a concerned and worried expression. This strategy demonstrates empathy, i.e. it shows the other person that we are listening and concerned	
	Tensing of muscles and trembling twitching hands could indicate rage or fear	

(Hayes 1984)

- *Performing.* This is the stage where the group gets down to work. Groups will differ on how long it takes them to get to this point. The degree to which groups work effectively together depends on how suitable and realistic their working plans are. Of course, if new difficulties emerge, then the group might well go back to the storming stage where they argue about how they are going to resolve these difficulties.
- *Adjourning.* At this point the task has been completed and the group prepares to disband. At this point there may be reflection or evaluation on how they worked together. If the group has worked well both academically and socially, the group could be upset at this stage. On the other hand if the group never managed to get on, the end will come as a relief and possibly lead to angry confrontations, where group members blame each other. What this means is that the way groups end needs to be managed (Leadbetter *et al.* 1999).

This is a very interesting model of group development and what it highlights is just how difficult it is to get a group of students to work effectively together.

Areas where tension can develop

Encouraging groups to work effectively can be difficult. The first step in encouraging effective group work is to be aware of issues facing groups and possible areas of conflict. Possible issues facing groups and signs of conflict to look out for include (Cohen *et al.* 1988):

- *Relationships.* Do group members spend more time arguing rather than working together? Or on the other hand, do some members get on too well and consequently other members feel left out?
- *Division of work.* Who does what? Who defines equal participation? Often groups spend time arguing over who does what. It is important to consider who assigns tasks. Does the group work this out together? Does the group pick a leader who assigns tasks? Does the teacher/teaching assistant set tasks or do they only intervene when it becomes apparent that the group cannot decide this for themselves. Groups are often concerned that everyone does their fair share of work. Possible problems could occur when there is an unfair division of work. The 'free rider effect' describes a situation where the less able students opt out and let the more able

students do all the work. The 'sucker effect' refers to the situation where the more able students become less involved as they feel that they are being taken advantage of. On the other hand the 'ganging up on the task' effect involves the entire group, or most of the group, deciding that they don't want to do the task (Bennett and Dunne 1992).

- *Ways of listening, communicating.* Do the individual members of the group know how to listen to each other? Do all members of the group contribute to group discussions equally? Do some members dominate the group while others are silent? Are all comments made by group members received with respect?
- *Understanding and acceptance of group goals.* Does the group under-stand what they should be doing? If the group does understand what they should be doing are they willing to do the task?
- *How to handle disagreements positively.* Who resolves group disagree-ments? Are the disagreements handled in a calm and reasoned manner, or does the disagreement quickly turn into a 'slanging match'? Can the group handle this by themselves, or does the teacher/teaching assistant need to intervene?

Another possible area of tension results when a teaching assistant is required to support both an individual within a group and the group itself. If a student has extensive needs, a teaching assistant might find it difficult to meet the needs of the individual student and the demands and requests for help from the rest of the group.

Now that we have mentioned many possible problems we need to move on to examine how we can resolve these issues. In the next section we talk about group dynamics, specifically highlighting strate-gies that help groups work together effectively.

Group dynamics and ways of resolving tensions in groups

Group dynamics explain how groups work together. Much research has been conducted on the conditions that make for effective groups or teams. Effective teams should:

- Have clearly defined roles and responsibilities.
- Agree on team and personal objectives.
- Encourage the involvement and participation of all team members.
- Have clear and established ways of communicating with each other.

In regard to working with students in groups, the first step that a teacher or a teaching assistant could take would be to establish ground rules for talking and listening. Groups of Year 2 students were asked to come up with between six and ten rules for working together. The groups suggested such ideas as 'Have ideas,' 'Don't be rude,' 'Keep trying,' 'Don't keep comments to yourself' and 'Help each other' (National Oracy Project 1990). Such ground rules can help create a positive working atmosphere.

Other ideas for training students in group-work skills involves giving students training in co-operation, self-monitoring and self-evaluation. Co-operation starts with concepts of how to get on with each other, as shown in the example of establishing ground rules, but then training in co-operation moves on to giving the students tasks where they have to learn how to work together in a positive and helpful manner. Kagan (1988) suggests assigning a task of colouring a group mural. The catch is that each student is allowed to use only one colour. This activity would involve the students working together to decide how they are going to complete this activity.

The next aspect of group work is **self-monitoring**, where each student is encouraged to monitor how they are doing and how the group is doing. As well as measuring progress on the task, they could also be encouraged to think about how they are getting on at a social level, i.e. how well are they listening and supporting each other.

The last aspect is **self-evaluation**, which takes place after the group has finished and asks the group to answer questions such as:

- Were all participants equally involved?
- How well did team members listen to and support each other?
- How were decisions made?
- What were the difficulties in working together and how were they resolved?
- What positive behaviours were seen in the group?
- Could the group have worked more effectively together and how?

Of course the above ideas will help groups, but there are times when a teacher or teaching assistant will need to intervene. Sometimes a group will need help in understanding what the task is. Sometimes they will need help in setting ground rules and help in resolving disagreements positively. The key here is to give the group ideas or ways of helping themselves. When trying to balance individual and group needs, sometimes it is helpful to work with the least able and get them started and then turn to the rest of the group. At this point an example would be of use.

Case study 6.2

Mike, a teaching assistant, was working in a special school and was coaching the Year 5 football team. Well, it was the first match of the year, it was half-time and they were behind by two goals. Things were not going well. Obviously the team was disappointed but what made it worse was that they were now arguing amongst themselves. Chris, who considered himself to be the real captain, was slagging off the goalie, saying that he was absolute crap and that so was the rest of the team. The goalie looked like he was either going to burst into tears or hit Chris. Mike took the team into the changing room and sat them all down in a circle. He said that he would ask them each in turn to make one suggestion that would lead to them playing better together. He said that they would each have their turn, and that no one would speak out of turn and that the suggestions must be positive. Mike was surprised about how well it went. Everyone had their say. The goalie said that he didn't want to be goalie and that he was much better as a forward. Another team member said he wanted to be goalie and most of them said that they would do much better if they took time to praise each other. They went back on to the pitch a much happier team and though they didn't win they did score a goal and were very pleased with the result.

Basic principles of effective working relationships with colleagues

Many of the principles we have discussed earlier about active listening and teamwork apply here. What this section will look at will be one specific theory that suggests ways to understand and improve relationships with colleagues.

Eric Berne (1968, 1991) developed a theory called **transactional analysis**. Berne was interested in how individuals communicate. He stated that every individual has three **ego states** and that when communicating with others an individual would talk from the perspective of one of these ego states. The three ego states are:

- *Parent.* This is the voice of authority. This ego state is our intern-alised parent. When we talk from the ego state of a parent, we tend to use words that are judgemental, critical and patronising, such as 'Don't,' 'I told you,' 'What did I say?'
- *Adult.* When we talk from an adult ego state, or from the perspective of an adult, we talk as a rational and thinking individual. We say things such as 'I think' and 'in my opinion'.
- *Child.* The child ego state is the emotional part of us. When we talk from the perspective of a child we might talk in a baby-like voice. We might be sulky, demanding, have a tantrum or be silly.

Of course this theory gets more complicated when you realise that not only do you have the option of talking from one of the three ego states, but the person you are talking to has the option of responding from one of their ego states. If you thought about all the conversations you have in a day you will realise that you use many ego states depending on the situation you are in and the person to whom you are talking. Let's look at the following examples.

TEACHING ASSISTANT (working on a computer with a student, nothing is going right, the computer has just crashed and all the student's work has been lost. Teaching assistant goes frantically up to the teacher): I am in a total muddle with the computer. It has just crashed and I don't know what to do next?

The teaching assistant is talking from a child ego state to the teacher's parent ego state.

TEACHER: Don't worry. I'll come over and sort it out right now.

The teacher is talking from a parent ego state to the teaching assistant's child ego state.

Later on in the day the teacher and the teaching assistant have the following conversation:

TEACHING ASSISTANT: Sam is having some difficulties with his reading book. Though he is still having some difficulties with the words, I think he is getting bored and frustrated. Perhaps it would be helpful to move him on to a different book.
TEACHER: I think that is a good idea. What do you think if we try him on . . .?

Here both the teaching assistant and the teacher are communicating on an adult to adult level, that is, they are both talking and responding from an adult ego state.

This theory comes in useful when trying to understand conversations that are difficult. Sometimes the difficulty lies in the fact that the person is talking to us in a format or way that we do not wish to be talked to. Let us look at another example. Jody is working in a Year 7 science class supporting two students who have difficulty with reading and writing. Jody sits with these students and sees her task as repeating instructions, as the students don't always follow what the teacher is saying. Sometimes Jody will act as a scribe and copies down notes for them. After one class the teacher called Jody over.

TEACHER: Now, Jody. You know that when I am talking in class I like the class to be completely quiet. Now I have noticed that you are often whispering to Sarah and Jason. I think that this is sending the wrong messages to the rest of the class.

JODY (rather sulkily): What do you want me to do?

TEACHER: Sit there and be quiet.

JODY: But the students I am supporting . . .

TEACHER: Not now, I am running late for a meeting. We will have to talk later.

Jody found this conversation difficult as she felt the teacher was not listening to her but treating her like a naughty child. In transactional terms the teacher was in a parent ego state and talking to her as a child. Jody responded as a sulky child – but what she wanted was to talk to the teacher and have the teacher talk to her on an adult to adult level. The next lesson Jody came early to class.

JODY: I would like to have a word with you about what we were talking about last time. Now, while I can see your point that talking to Sarah and Jason is sending the wrong messages, I also think that without some sort of feedback in class Sarah and Jason are not going to cope with the demands of the lesson. I would like to talk over some alternative strategies where I could give Sarah and Jason feedback, but in a way that would not be disruptive to your lesson.

Here Jody is talking to the teacher from an adult ego state to an adult ego state in the hope that the teacher will respond likewise.

In general, when working with colleagues an adult ego state to adult ego state conversation or transaction is desirable. Talking in this manner communicates respect and encourages co-operation and teamwork.

This method can also be used in communication with students, especially older students. When you as the teaching assistant talk to the students as if they were an adult from an adult perspective; what you are hoping is that they will respond on a similar level.

Reflective component

Case study 6.3: secondary school

Joanne works in a secondary school and this is how she describes one particularly difficult day.

Description of event (What happened? What should have happened?)

I was supporting two students, Amy and Sarah, in history. The task of the class was to write a letter home from the perspective of a World War I soldier who was fighting in the trenches. Both Amy and Sarah found this task difficult. I would try to get them started but when I left them to see other students they would just talk between themselves about what they were going to do on the weekend, who was going to see whom and what they should wear. In the end they achieved absolutely nothing in class. After class I had a chat with Amy. I told her that I was disappointed in her behaviour as I knew she could do better. I asked her what she thought she could do to improve. She said that she thought she would work better if she was not sitting next to Sarah. I said I thought that was a good idea and that I would mention it to the teacher. Well, later that afternoon as school was finishing I saw Sarah in the corridor. She came up to me with tears in her eyes and said: 'I hate you. I thought you were my friend. It is because of you that I can't sit beside Amy any more,' and with that she ran down the hall and out of the school.

Self-assessment

Your task is to complete the reflective log. Remember to use the headings: *Feelings* (How did you feel? How do you think the students felt?), *Evaluation* (What was good? What was difficult?), *Analysis* (How do you make sense of this?), *In conclusion* (What else could you have done?), *Action plan* (What will you do next?). Hint: consider some of the strategies we have talked about in this chapter.

Case study 6.4: primary school

Jane was working in a junior school with Year 5. The class was doing the Victorians. The group task was to write a newspaper report about a famous event that occurred during the reign of Queen Victoria. However, things were not going to plan, as Jane writes.

Description of event

Emily was upset as she was not in the same group as her best friend, Amanda. Robert and Charles were together and though most days they got on really well, today they were not talking to each other.

I suggested that as a group they should first read a summary of the key events from the reign of Queen Victoria and then decide what to write about. Of course it would be a good idea if they took turns reading.

Charles started. However, Charles had only read one paragraph when Emily said in a loud voice that reading out loud was stupid and a waste of time and if that was what they were going to do, well, then they could count her out, because she was not going to read.

I asked Emily to go sit at another table by herself until she could learn to behave in a reasonable manner.

I asked the group what they felt about Emily's statement. Should she be allowed to get out of reading? Charles said: 'Well, none of us like reading, so I don't see why she should get out of it.' I said that Emily found it difficult to read and that they should be supportive when she read.

I went over to Emily and explained that she could come back to the group, but she would have to read and that the other students would be supportive. Emily did come back and when it was her turn to read the group was very encouraging.

Next it was time to decide what to do. The problem was that everyone wanted to do the title page and no one wanted to write the newspaper article. This caused such a heated debate that I could not hear myself think. Luckily the class was over, but the lesson would be continued the next day.

Self-assessment

Your task is to complete the reflective log. Remember to use the headings. Hint: consider some of the strategies we have talked about in this chapter.

Chapter 7

Promoting independence and self-esteem

Definitions of self-esteem and self-concept

We all carry around with us an image of who we are, who we have been and the type of person we have the possibility of becoming. Psychologists have spent much time researching in this area. At this point it is helpful to look at some definitions. Lawrence (1996) feels that there are three aspects of the self:

- *Behaviour.* What we do. How we present ourselves to others.
- *Affect.* How we feel about ourselves.
- *Cognition.* How we think about ourselves.

Lawrence (1996) further states that **self-concept**, the entirety of who we are, the total person, can be divided into **self-image**, **ideal self** and **self-esteem.** These terms are defined as:

- *Self-image.* How an individual describes themselves in terms of physical and mental characteristics (e.g. how thin, tall, clever, artistic, gorgeous, are we?).
- *Ideal self.* What an individual would like to be or have in terms of physical and mental characteristics.
- *Self-esteem.* The difference between the self-image and the ideal self, that is, the difference between the way we see ourselves and the way we would like to be. Whether we have a high or low self-esteem depends on our evaluation of ourselves. The greater the difference between self image and ideal self, the lower the self-esteem.

Harter (1982) talked about four areas where we could evaluate ourselves, these being:

- *Cognitive competence.* How intelligent are we?
- *Social competence.* How popular are we?
- *Physical competence.* How good at sports or games are we?
- *General self-worth.* How good a person do we feel we are?

Factors that affect the development of self-esteem and self-concept

Our concept of self develops over time. Certainly a young baby would not have a self-concept but a fifteen-year-old would. Cooley (1902) put forward a **looking-glass theory** to explain how the self concept developed. Cooley (1902) believed that we look to others in order to define ourselves. So, in a sense, our self is a reflection of 'how we think others see us'. Mead (1934), expanding on Cooley's views, stated that with time the views of how other specific people see us becomes internalised into a general view of how all other people see us. Mead (1934) also felt that the self was constantly being defined and redefined through the everyday interactions and conversations we have with others. Everyday interactions are important, as it is in these interactions that we make comparisons between ourselves and other people.

The ability of becoming aware of how other people see us and our ability to make comparisons between ourselves and others develops with time. Pre-schoolers truly believe that they are the greatest and the best and this belief exists even when it is obvious that they are not (Frey and Ruble 1985). For example, a four-year-old might believe he can run as fast as a speeding bullet, even though he has just come last in the running race. However, by the age of six, children are able to make social comparisons. If you ask a child of six whether they are a good reader they might say, 'Well, Emma is better at reading than me because she is on the blue book, however I am better than Sam, because he is still on the red books.' As children become older they become increasingly attentive to social comparisons (picking up on teachers' and parents' looks and tone of voice) and more subtle in regard to finding out how others have done.

Research has been carried out in regard to gender differences in self-esteem and self-worth. A study by the American Association of University Women (Sadker and Sadker 1994) found that boys and girls have similar levels of self-esteem in primary and junior schools, though in general females drop in levels of self-esteem relative to males during secondary school. Kwa (1994) found that having a good physical appearance was the strongest predictor of self-worth in females, whereas males felt valued for how their bodies performed in athletic activities.

Social factors can influence self-concept and self-esteem. Social factors relate to the value that society places on performing certain activities, occupying certain roles or jobs and possessing certain physical traits. Society values individuals who excel at sports, individuals who gain leadership roles (e.g. head girl, head boy, captain of the football team) and society values individuals who possess physical attributes such as beauty. Within the last twenty years the incidence of adolescents with eating disorders has risen dramatically. Though boys do suffer from eating disorders, females make up the majority of sufferers, with younger and younger girls becoming worried about weight. Society celebrates the supermodel and sadly many girls aspire to this ideal.

Though we can say that English culture as a whole values certain characteristics and traits, England is now a multi-racial and multi-ethnic society. Sometimes sub-cultures will have values that conflict with the culture at large. Juvenile gangs could be considered a sub-culture. Certainly within these sub-cultures respect for authority and academic excellence would not be seen as valued.

An important concept in this area is the issue of labelling. Rosenthal and Jacobson (1966) conducted a classic study in this area on the effects of teacher expectations and what they termed **self-fulfilling prophecies**. The researchers went into a school and gave an intelligence test to all students. The researchers then told the teachers that on the basis of the test results they had identified certain students who were 'academic bloomers', that is, students who would really come on in leaps and bounds in the forthcoming academic year. At the end of the year they went back to the school and administered another intelligence test to all the students. They discovered that these 'academic bloomers' had indeed increased in intelligence. However, the catch is that the researchers had lied to the teachers at the beginning of the year. There were no 'academic bloomers'; the researchers had just chosen students' names randomly from the school register. The important aspect of this study was that the students whom the teachers thought would improve academically did. Why did this happen? Perhaps the students improved simply because the teachers thought they would. Perhaps the teachers spent more time with these students. Perhaps the teachers encouraged them and praised them more. But what this study does show is the power of teacher expectations and that students can live up to (as in this study) or live down to expectations.

Strategies that will enhance self-esteem

What has been said in the previous section has important implications for working with students in schools. There are several key points:

- Students develop a self-concept through their interactions with others. In terms of a school environment this includes other students and the teaching staff.
- Students will observe how others see them and react by internalising this into a view regarding how 'others think of me'. So, if others see me as thick and naughty, in time that is how I see myself.
- Students will draw social comparisons between themselves and other students.
- Students as they become older become very good at picking up subtle clues in social interactions. Students will pick up on tone of voice, the use of sarcasm, various looks, etc.

What all this means is that, in order to boost a student's self-esteem, a teaching assistant must always be aware of how they are reacting to the student and be aware of damaging interactions between students.

General strategies for interacting with students are:

- Try to think positively about all the students you work with. Try to deal with even the difficult students in a positive manner.
- Make a point of telling the students what their strengths are.
- Communicate to the student that you like them and value them.
- Praise students regularly but ensure that the praise is genuine.
- Give them tasks that they can succeed in.
- If they don't succeed, find some aspect of the task that they have done well.
- Tell the student about your mistakes. Tell them how you have learned through your mistakes. Tell them how you felt when you failed at something. Tell them how you dealt with failure by trying harder. Tell them we all make mistakes.
- Encourage students to be supportive of each other.

Of course these suggestions sound good but how do you do it in the real classroom environment? Imagine the following scene.

Everyone in the Year 9 maths class is settling down to do their work – that is, with the exception of James. James is slouched in his chair; he has not brought in his maths textbook or his workbook, nor does he have any pens or paper. James looks bored and defiant and is chewing gum noisily. As the teaching assistant you have given him some paper and a pen yet he has still not started to work though you have asked him twice. What do you say next?

- 'James, I have had enough of you. You never bring in your books. You will never pass your exams at this rate and as for your chewing gum, well, that's about the only thing you can do' *or*
- 'James, you are an intelligent boy, why are you still just sitting there? If you don't know where to begin you know, you just have to ask me.'

However, though you can do all you can to encourage an atmosphere of respect for all students and remind students of the school behaviour charter, students can be at times very cruel to each other. Sometimes in these cases it is recommended that you work with the students to develop an internal sense of self-worth. For example one activity (Canfield 1994) has the teacher instruct the students to learn by heart the following phrase: 'No matter what you say or do to me, I am still a worthwhile person.'

Factors that promote independence

The ultimate aim of an education system is give the student a thirst for acquiring knowledge and the necessary skills in order to do so. This view sees learning as a lifelong process. While in the early years learning is very much guided by the teaching staff it is expected that students going on to college and university will have become independent learners. Independent learners:

- Know what they need to do in order to complete the assignment or answer the question.
- Know how to ask for help.
- Know how to gather the needed information.
- Know how to present ideas.
- Know how to use their time effectively.
- Know how to review and evaluate their own work against what they have been asked to achieve.

- Take responsibility for their learning.

It is obvious that these skills are of value. But how are they learned? Some students will naturally pick these skills up, while others will need to be taught these skills in a step-by-step approach.

Strategies designed to encourage independence

Factors that will encourage independent learning are:

- Specific study skills programmes that aim to teach students how to study effectively give students the skills to become independent learners. One such programme that we have talked about (see p. 58) is process-based instruction. This programme teaches skills such as where to start, what actions are needed, how to monitor work and how to review or verify whether work has been completed. Another programme is Robinson's SQ3R method of effective reading.
- Encouraging choice and decision-making skills encourages independent learning by creating in the student a sense of ownership, responsibility and pride in their work.

Robinson SQ3R method of effective reading

This method is ideally suited to older students who will use textbooks and other reading resources for research purposes.

- *Survey.* Before reading the chapter try to get an overview of what material the chapter is presenting. Looking at chapter outlines and various headings in the text will help.
- *Question.* For every heading in the text convert it into a question. Asking questions helps the student to become involved in the learning process.
- *Read.* Read one section of the text at a time with the goal of answering the question.
- *Recite.* After reading the section, answer in your own words the question you have formed. Sometimes it is helpful to do this out loud. At this point the student could be encouraged to make some notes.
- *Review.* When the student has finished the chapter then they can review the key notes that they have made.

Teaching choice and decision-making skills

Before we go any further it is important to define our terms. What do we mean by choice and decision making? *Choice* has been defined as the act of making a selection of a preferred alternative from among several options (Shevin and Klein 1984). So a choice involves selecting an option from several possibilities. *Decision making* is defined as a process which involves a reasonable amount of thinking that is focused on deciding what to believe and do (Ennis 1987). In this book we have previously talked about making the student aware that they have choices regarding how they behave. But what other decisions and choices do students have?

- Students can choose what books to read.
- Students can choose what resources they want to use. A student at a primary level working on a maths worksheet might have a choice between using a number line or counters.
- Students might be given a choice in regard to what to do for a project, an essay or coursework.
- Students can choose to go to homework club.
- Students can select what extra activity clubs they join.

We have discussed some choices that students have, but how can a teacher or teaching assistant encourage or facilitate choice and decision-making opportunities? The following suggestions have been seen to be helpful:

- Give students realistic choices.
- In order to make a choice, the students need to know what the options are and to have some sort of experience of what the options involve. For example a student cannot realistically make a choice to attend a homework club if they do not know what a homework club entails.
- Do not give too many choices, as this can overwhelm the students.
- Support and respect the choices and decisions that students have made.
- Help students to evaluate their choices and decisions by asking questions.

When considering giving choices and allowing students to make decisions, the question most teachers and teaching assistants have is what to do when the student does not make the right choice. Consider the following example.

Judy, a teaching assistant in a junior school, supports Dan, who has difficulties in reading and spelling. Every week Dan can choose a book that he can read with the teaching assistant. What Judy has noticed is that every week Dan always goes for the easy option. Dan always chooses books that he can read easily. Therefore his choice does not teach or extend his reading abilities. What can Judy do? Dan has made his choice. However, Judy could ask Dan to evaluate for himself how easy he found the book and ask him whether he thinks he could choose a book that was somewhat more challenging.

Reflective component

Case study 7.1: primary school

Nancy works in a primary school.

Description of event (What happened?)

The teacher had asked the class to write a poem on 'Rain'. The teacher asked me to go round the class and help any students who were having problems. Well, I was very impressed with the children's work. I stopped and read Robert's poem. It was lovely. I said to Robert what a lovely poem it was, but instead of being pleased he said 'No it's not' and proceeded to rip the paper up. Well, it was time for break and Robert went out with all the other students. I had a word with the teacher, as I really did not know what to make of Robert's behaviour. The teacher seemed just as puzzled as I was.

Feelings (What did I feel? What do I think the student(s) were feeling?)

Well, I was very upset by what had happened and of course Robert was as well.

Self-assessment

Your task is to complete the reflective log from the perspective of the teaching assistant. Remember to use the headings: *Evaluation* (What was good? What was difficult?), *Analysis* (How do you make sense of this?), *In conclusion* (What else could you have done?), *Action plan* (What would you do next time?). Hint: consider the theories and strategies that have been mentioned in this chapter.

Case study 7.2: secondary school

Sarah describes the following.

Description of event (What happened?)

I was supporting a number of students in a maths class. At the end of the lesson I was going around the class quickly checking students' work. I looked at Amy's worksheet. I noticed that there were a number of mistakes. I said to Amy, 'Shall we check this over together?' Amy said, 'There is no need! I am brilliant at maths!' Well, the bell went at that moment.

Feelings (What did I feel? What did I think the student(s) were feeling?)

I was at a loss as to how to deal with Amy. Amy was so convinced that she was right and she was so happy to have finished the whole worksheet.

Self-assessment

Your task is to complete the reflective log from the perspective of the teaching assistant. Remember to use the headings. Hint: consider the theories and strategies that have been mentioned in this chapter.

The content of the book mapped on to the National Occupational Standards and other qualifications

Chapter	National Occupational Standards	City and Guilds	Cache
Introduction	Unit 3.4	Elements 9, 12, 13	
1 Basic principles underlying pupil development and learning	Units 2.3, 2.5, 3.1, 3.3, 3.8, 3.12, 3.18, 3.19	Elements 3, 5, 6, 8, 17, 18, 23, 24	CTA (2) Unit 1 CTA (3) Unit 2
2 Learning support strategies	Units 2.3, 2.5, 3.3, 3.8, 3.18, 3.19, 3.20	Elements 3, 5, 8, 12, 23, 24	CTA (2) Unit 1 CTA (3) Unit 2
3 Learning styles	Units 2.5, 3.3, 3.5, 3.8	Elements 7, 8, 25, 23	CTA (2) Unit 1 CTA (3) Unit 2
4 Pupils with special needs	Units 2.5, 3.8, 3.12, 3.13, 3.14, 3.15, 3.16	Elements 17, 18, 19, 20, 21	CTA (2) Unit 1 CTA (3) Unit 2
5 Preventing and managing emotional/ behavioural difficulties	Units 3.1, 3.15	Elements 6, 20	CTA (2) Unit 2 CTA (3) Unit 2
6 Establishing effective working relationships with pupils and colleagues	Units 2.4, 3.2, 3.3, 3.9, 3.21, 3.22	Elements 4, 7, 14, 26, 27	CTA (2) Unit 2 CTA (3) Unit 1 CTA (3) Unit 3
7 Promoting independence and self-esteem	Units 3.1, 3.9, 3.14, 3.15	Elements 6, 8, 14, 17, 21,	CTA (2) Unit 2 CTA (3) Unit 1 CTA (3) Unit 3

Useful contacts and resources

Journals

Special Children
Questions Publishing Company. www.education-quest.com

Topic
NFER, The Mere, Upton Park, Slough, Berks SL1 2OQ
Practical applications of research in education (on-line and printed)

Useful contacts

ADD Information Services
PO Box 340, Edgware, Middlesex HA8 9HL
AFASIC (Association for all Speech Impaired Children)
347 Central Markets, Smithfield, London EC1A 9NH
BILD (British Institute of Learning Disabilities)
Campion House, Green Street, Kidderminster, Worcestershire
DY10 1JL. www.bild.org.uk
DfES (Department for Education and Skills)
www.dfes.gov.uk/sen. Government site with information on
policies and updates regarding special educational needs
Down's Syndrome News and Update
Down's Syndrome Educational Trust, The Sarah Duffen Centre,
Belmont Street, Southsea, Portsmouth, Hampshire PO5 1NA
Dyslexia Institute
133 Gresham Road, Staines, Middlesex TW18 2AJ. www.dyslexia-
inst.org.uk
Dyspraxia Foundation
8 West Alley, Hitchin, Hertfordshire SG5 IEG

NASEN (National Association for Special Educational Needs)
NASEN House, 4/5 Amber Business Village, Amber Close, Tamworth, Staffordshire B77 4RP. www.nasen.org.uk
NFER (National Foundation for Educational Research)
   The Mere, Upton Park, Slough, Berkshire SL1 2OQ. www.nfer. ac.uk/
OAASIS (Office for Advice, Assistance, Support and Information on Special Needs)
   Brock House, Grigg Lane, Brockenhurst, Hampshire SO42 7RE. www.oaasis.co.uk
National Autistic Society
   393 City Road, Stratford, London EC1V 1NG. www.nas.org.uk

Glossary

The first occurrence of each of these terms is highlighted by bold in the main text.

Accommodation   A term used by Piaget to describe how individuals change or modify schemas to incorporate new experiences.

Active listening   A special type of listening where we communicate to the person whom we are talking with that we have indeed heard and understood what they have said.

Adaptation   According to Piaget adaptation describes the changes an individual makes in response to the environment. The changes involve the development of schemas through the processes of assimilation and accommodation.

ADHD   Attention Deficit Hyperactivity Disorder is cited by the *DSM* IV as a condition marked by excessive activity, impulsiveness and problems in regard to sustained attention.

Assimilation   A Piagetian term to describe how new information is fitted into existing schemas.

Auditory learners prefer to learn through hearing and listening to material.

Autism/Autistic Spectrum Disorder   A condition characterised by problems in social interaction, communication, imaginative activity combined with a limited range of activities and interests. Autism is now commonly referred to Autistic Spectrum Disorder (ASD).

Basic interpersonal communication skills   The language first learned by toddlers and pre-schoolers. In acquiring a second language it is thought to take from one to two years to achieve this level of competence.

Behavioural analysis The process of trying to understand and explain a person's behaviour.

Biological maturation describes how an individual changes and develops with age.

Bottom-up processing involves using our knowledge of basic principles to help us process material. An example of bottom-up processing would be using the knowledge of letter/sound combinations to help us to read.

Braille A tactile system of communication consisting of raised dots corresponding to letters of the alphabet. This system is used by individuals with sensory impairment.

Classical conditioning involves associating the automatic reactions caused by one event to other events that just happen to be occurring at the same time.

Cochlear implants are a type of hearing aid that relies on sending electrical signals directly to the auditory nerve to provide a sense of hearing.

Cognitive academic language proficiency The language used within classroom contexts and the standard necessary to cope with GCSEs. In acquiring a second language it is thought to take from five to seven years to achieve this level of competence.

Cognitive development The development of intellectual processes to include thinking, knowing, reasoning, understanding and problem solving.

Cognitive disequilibrium An unpleasant mental state that results when an individual realises that they cannot fit new experiences into existing schemas. In everyday language, an individual becomes confused when they realise they don't understand.

Co-morbidity The degree to which one health condition is associated with another condition.

Conditioned emotional responses A type of learning that results in certain events and situations being associated with particular emotions and feelings.

Conditioned response A term used in explaining the process of classical conditioning. A response elicited by a conditioned stimulus.

Conditioned stimulus A term used in explaining the process of classical conditioning. A stimulus, which initially does not elicit any reflex response, but comes to do so by being paired with an unconditioned stimulus.

Conserve A term used by Piaget to describe the child's awareness that an object will only have changed if something has been added or subtracted. Once the child has developed the ability to conserve, they will not be fooled by visual appearances.

Constructive feedback is a type of feedback that both acknowledges what still needs to be done and what has been done but in a manner that is seen as helpful and positive by the individual receiving the feedback.

Critical period hypothesis A belief held by certain theorists that the earlier a language is learnt the easier it is, and that it is easier to learn a language before puberty than after.

Decentre A Piagetian term to describe a child's ability to hold and understand in their mind, multiple and sometimes opposing views. For example, two lumps of play-dough of the same weight still weigh the same even if they have been rolled into different shapes and therefore do not look the same.

Deferred imitation The ability to imitate or copy a behaviour after a period of time has passed.

Developmental Co-ordination Disorder refers to problems in motor co-ordination experienced by a child that cannot be explained by a gneral medical condition. Also known as Dyspraxia.

Discovery learning An approach which sees an individual's active participation in a learning activity as being responsible for the development of new knowledge.

Down's syndrome A chromosomal anomaly resulting in there being forty-seven chromosomes in each cell instead of forty-six. An extra chromosome 21 is responsible for this condition.

Dyslexia Difficulty learning to read and spell despite adequate intelligence, instruction and opportunity.

Dyspraxia A condition marked by problems with motor co-ordination. Dyspraxia is also known as Developmental Co-ordination Disorder.

Echolalia is a condition where an individual repeats words or phrases that they heard others say. However, this repetition, is not used as a form of communication with others. This condition is often found in individuals with autism.

Egocentrism/Egocentric Terms used by Piaget to describe the tendency of a young child to believe that others see things from their perspective.

Ego states   A term used by Eric Berne in his theory of transactional analysis. According to the theory each individual has three ego states or perspectives from which they communicate to others. The three ego states are parent, adult and child.

Emotional behavioural difficulties   Behaviour which challenges and/or causes concern to the teacher.

Emotional intelligence   Being aware of, managing and using one's own emotions productively. Emotional intelligence also involves the ability to read and understand others' emotions and the art of dealing effectively with all aspects of social relationships.

Encoding   The process of transforming incoming information into a form that can be stored in memory.

Expressive language   The extent to which an individual can communicate.

Fine motor skills   Refined movements using only certain body parts, i.e. handwriting.

Gaze monitoring   The ability to follow another person's gaze, i.e. the ability to know what another person is looking at.

General symbolic function   According to Piaget one of the main accomplishments of the sensori-motor stage of development. This accomplishment includes the development of language, deferred imitation and make-believe play.

Grapheme–phoneme awareness   Graphemes refer to the letters of the alphabet, while phonemes refers to particular sound units. Grapheme–phoneme awareness thus refers to the knowledge of which letters or combinations of letters are associated with which sounds.

Graphemes   A written symbol of a language system, i.e. letters of the alphabet.

Gross motor skills   Physical movements that involve the whole body, i.e. jumping.

Group dynamics   The interactions that take place within a group.

Group socialisation theory as argued by Harris (1997) states that it is the social/peer group an individual belongs to that determines their behaviour.

Holophrases   A stage in early language development where one word in combination with gestures is used to communicate the meaning usually expressed in one sentence. Holophrases are one word sentences.

Hyperlexia A condition where a child's reading skills greatly surpass their comprehension skills, i.e. an individual can fluently read a passage of text but not understand what they have just read.

Hypothetical deductive reasoning A type of reasoning that emerges in Piaget's formal operational stage. Individuals of 11 and above have an understanding of hypotheses, which involves creating, noting implications, testing, drawing conclusions and from the analysis of conclusions creating yet more hypotheses.

Ideal self The person who we would like to be, i.e. the physical and mental characteristics we would like to have.

Ideational A type of dyspraxia that refers to individuals who have difficulty in planning a sequence of co-ordinated movements.

Ideo-motor A type of dyspraxia that refers to individuals who know what they want to do, the right sequence of movements, but have difficulties in executing these movements. These individuals may appear clumsy or awkward.

Intelligence tests Tests administered by educational or clinical psychologist to mesure cognitive or intellectual ability.

Interaction in the environment describes how and to what exten the individual is involved with what is happening around them.

Instrumental pointing Babies use pointing to communicate. Instrumental pointing communicates the need to have an object. The baby points to the object because they want to have that object.

Intrinsic Stemming from within the person.

Kinaesthetic learners prefer to learn through physical movement and hands-on activities.

Language acquisition device Some theorists believe that there is 'something' within our brain that we are born with, an innate mental mechanism, that allows us to develop language, specifically grammar.

Learning style An individual's preference in regard to how they wish to learn new information.

Looking-glass theory developed by Cooley (1902) states that we look to others in order to define who we are.

Maturational readiness The age or stage of development when a child will be ready and able to learn new knowledge.

Memory strategy is that 'something special' that we need to do to unrelated information in order to remember it.

Metamemory   Knowledge about memory, in particular one's own memory abilities.

Moon   A tactile system of communication based on raised letters that are similar to the letters of the alphabet as we know them. This system is used with individuals with both sensory impairments and general learning disabilities.

Motherese   A style of language used by an adult when talking to a baby or young child. This language is characterised by shorter, grammatically simple sentences spoken at a higher pitch and at a slower pace.

Multi-sensory rooms are designed for individuals with multiple disabilities. Multi-sensory rooms offer the individual a range of sensory experiences involving sight, sound, touch and smell. Some of these experiences can be controlled by the individual with disabilities by the use of specially designed switches.

Multi-sensory techniques are often used in the teaching of phonics. This technique aims to teach through an approach that uses all senses, auditory, visual and kinaesthetic.

Non-verbal communication involves communication with others through the use of eye contact, tone of voice and body movements.

Objects of reference are specific objects that have a meaning assigned to them. Objects of reference are used as a system of communication with individuals who have multiple disabilities.

Object permanence   A Piagetian term describing the realisation that objects continue to exist in time and space regardless of whether an individual can see them or not.

Occupational therapists   Occupational therapists are involved in the assessment and treatment of disorders of movement. Occupational therapists are interested in assessing what daily living skills an individual has and providing suitable equipment and adaptations to the individuals environment so thta they can be as independent as possible.

Over-regularisation/Over-generalisation   A stage in early grammar development where the child will apply known existing rules of grammar to all words. At this stage the child will not know that certain words are exceptions to the rule. A child at this stage might say: 'I hurted'.

Perceptual style   How students take in and process information, specifically what senses are being used. Students will show preferences in regard to what senses they use to process information. (See Visual learners, Auditory learners, Kinaesthetic learners.)

Phonemes Distinct sound units, which in combination form words.

Physiotherapists Physiotherapists are involved in the assessment and treatment of disorders of movement. Physiotherapists use treatments such as exercise, heat and manipulation.

Picture Exchange Communication System (PECS) An intervention used with individuals who have difficulties with language and communication. To begin with a student is required to exchange a picture of a desired object for the object itself. This system using picture cards (pictures represent objects) encourages an individual to communicate by creating combinations of pictures corresponding to sentences.

Probes Follow up questions designed to elicit more specific information.

Process-based instruction A strategy devised by Ashman and Conway (1993) that teaches students how to solve problems and plan their work.

Prompts are follow-up questions given to a student, when the answer received is not quite the answer you are looking for. The aim of a prompt is to help the student give the desired answer.

Proprioceptive system refers to a type of receptor that is present in the muscles and joints that enables an individual to be aware of body position and to move without visual guidance.

Prosopagnosia A rare condition where individuals have no problem seeing faces, but have difficulties making sense of faces. An individual with such a condition could meet a close relative on the street and not recognise them.

Proto-declarative pointing Babies use pointing to communicate. This communication is not based on a desire to have an object but more a desire to share an experience.

Receptive language How much an individual can understand of what is being said to them.

Repetitive routines Repetitive routines are daily events in a child's life, i.e. getting dressed or having a bath. In the course of these repetitive routines, parents often use the same language. This repetition of the same language in the same context helps the child to break the code of language.

Resilience factors are those situations, events, relationships, personality traits that serves to protect an individual from negative conditions, such as mental health probelms.

Retrieval describes the process of how we access stored information.

Risk factors are those situations, events, relationships, personality traits that increases the chances that an individual will experience negative conditions, such as mental health problems.

Scaffolding   A concept used by Vygotsky and expanded upon by Bruner to describe the process of help by which a more skilled individual teaches a less skilled individual.

Schemas   Organised patterns or units of action or thought that we construct to make sense of our interactions with the world.

Self-concept   Defined as the whole person. The self-concept can be divided into the self-image, the ideal self and self-esteem.

Self-esteem   The extent to which one values oneself.

Self-evaluation involves the individual making a judgement regarding aspects of their behaviour.

Self-fulfilling prophecy   The tendency for things to turn out as expected. For example a teacher who expects a student to fail might treat the student in a manner that increases the likelihood that they will fail. In this example the teacher's expectations have come true, but the student's failure is in part due to the teacher's behaviour.

Self-image   How an individual describes themselves.

Self-monitoring involves the individual being aware of exactly how they are engaging in an activity.

Sequential bilingual acquisition involves an individual first learning one language and then at some later stage being introduced to a second language.

Simultaneous bilingual acquisition   A situation where a child, from infancy, will learn two languages at the same time.

Social learning theory states that we learn by observing and imitating others.

Spiral curriculum   A concept used by Bruner which sees concepts being developed and redeveloped with increasing levels of complexity as the child progresses through the education system.

Storage   Once information is encoded then it needs to be stored for future use. The form of storage according to Piaget is units of mental thought called schemas.

Tactile receptors are specialised cells within the skin that sends information about light, touch, pain, temperature and pressure to the brain.

Task analysis Breaking a task or a skill into steps or component parts. Once the smaller steps or parts have been identified it is possible to determine what steps or parts the student can do and what steps or parts they cannot do.

Telegraphic speech A stage in early language development where the child will use only key words to express themselves.

Theory of mind The ability to guess what other people are thinking and feeling. An individual who has this ability can use it to make sense of and predict other individuals' behaviour.

Top-down processing involves using our knowledge of the world, what happens in the world and our knowledge of spoken language to help us process material, i.e. to help us to read.

Transactional analysis A theory developed by Eric Berne. Berne was interested in how individuals communicate with each other. From this theory Berne devised a therapy to enhance communication.

Transitivity A type of reasoning involved in answering questions such as: 'If Joe is taller than Sam, and Sam is taller than Rob, who is tallest, Joe or Rob?'

Unconditioned response A term used in explaining the process of classical conditioning. A reflex response that is elicited by an unconditioned stimulus.

Unconditioned stimulus A term used in explaining the process of classical conditioning. A stimulus that has the natural ability to evoke a reflex response.

Vestibular apparatus referes to receptors that are located within the inner ear that automatically co-ordinates movements of the eyes, head, ears and body in order to maintain balance.

Visual learners prefer to learn through seeing and watching.

Zone of Proximal Development Vygotsky referred to this as the difference between what individuals could achieve by themselves and what they could achieve with assistance. Vygotsky saw this difference as measuring individuals' potential to learn.

Bibliography

APA (1995) *Diagnostic and Statistical Manual of Mental Disorders*, 4th edn, Washington DC: American Psychological Association

Ashman, A. and Conway, R. (1993) *Using Cognitive Methods in the Classroom*, London: Routledge

Atkinson, R. L., Atkinson, R. C., Smith, E. E. and Bem, D. J. (1993) *Introduction to Psychology*, 11th edn, New York: Harcourt Brace

Bailey, M. (1967) 'The utility of phonic generalisations in Grades One through Six', *Reading Teacher*, 20, 413–18

Bandura, A. (1977) *Social Learning Theory*, Morristown NJ: General Learning Press

Barkley, R. A. (1998) 'Attention Deficit Hyperactivity Disorder', *Scientific American*, September, 44–9

Baron-Cohen, S., Leslie, A. M. and Frith, U. (1985) 'Does the autistic child have a "theory of mind"?' *Cognition*, 21, 37–46

Barrs, M., Ellis, S., Hester, H. and Kelly, A. V. (1988) *The Primary Language Record Handbook*, London: CLPE

Bell, A. W.; Kuchemann, D. and Costello, J. (1983) *A Review of Research in Mathematical Education:* Part A, *Teaching and Learning*, Windsor: NFER-Nelson

Bennett, N. and Dunne, E. (1992) *Managing Classroom Groups*, Hemel Hempstead: Simon and Schuster

Berko Gleason, J. (1997) *The Development of Language*, 4th edn, Boston MA: Allyn and Bacon

Berne, E. (1968) *Games People Play*, London: Penguin Books

Berne, E. (1991) *Transactional Analysis in Psychotherapy*, London: Souvenir Press

Bondy, A. S. and Frost, L. A. (1994) 'The Picture Exchange Communication System', *Focus on Autistic Behaviour*, 9 (3), 1–19

British Stammering Association (1997) *A Chance to Speak: Helping a Pupil who Stammers: A Practical Guide for Teachers*, London: BSA

Brown, G. and Wragg, E. C. (1993) *Questioning*, London: Routledge

Bruner, J. S. (1963) *The Process of Education*, Cambridge MA: Harvard University Press

Bruner, J. (1983) *Child's Talk: Learning to Use Language*, New York: Norton

Buckley, S. (1993) 'Language development in children with Down's syndrome: reasons for optimism', *Down's Syndrome: Research and Practice*, 1 (1), 3–9

Buckley, S. (1995) 'Improving the expressive language skills of teenagers with Down's syndrome', *Down's Syndrome: Research and Practice*, 3 (3), 110–15

Buckley, S. (1996) 'Reading before talking: learning about mental abilities from children with Down's syndrome', *The University of Portsmouth Inaugural Lectures*, 9 May.

Buckley, S. and Bird, G. (1993) 'Teaching children with Down's syndrome to read', *Down's Syndrome: Research and Practice*, 1 (1), 34–9

Canfield, J. (1994) *100 Ways to Enhance Self-concept in the Classroom: A Handbook for Teachers*, 2nd edn, Boston MA: Allyn and Bacon

Carter, R. (1998) *Mapping the Mind*, London: Weidenfeld and Nicolson

Charlton, T. and David, K. (eds) (1993) *Managing Misbehaviour in Schools*, London: Routledge

Chomsky, N. (1965) *Aspects of the Theory of Syntax*, Cambridge MA: MIT Press

Cohen, A. R., Fink, S. L, Gadon, H. and Willits, R. D. (1988) *Effective Behaviour in Organizations*, 4th edn, Homewood IL: Irwin

Conrad, K., Cermak, S. A. and Drake, C. (1983) 'Differentiation of praxis among children', *American Journal of Occupational Therapy*, 37, 466–73

Cooley, C. H. (1902) *Human Nature and the Social Order*, New York: Scribner's

Cowen, E. L., Pederson, A., Babigian, H., Izzo, L. D. and Trost, M. A. (1973) 'Long-term follow-up of early detected vulnerable children', *Journal of Consulting and Clinical Psychology*, 41, 438–46

Critchley, M. (1970) *The Dyslexic Child*, Springfield IL: Thomas

Cummins, J. (1984) *Bilingualism and Special Education: Issues in Assessment and Pedagogy*. San Diego CA: College Hill Press

Daniels, H., Visser, J., Cole, T. and Reybekill, N. de (1999) *Emotional and Behavioural Difficulties in Mainstream Schools*. School of Education, University of Birmingham, DfEE, RR90

Department for Education and Science (1981) *The Education Act*, London: HMSO

Department for Education and Skills (2001) *Special Educational Needs: Code of Practice*, Annesley: DfES Publications

Detweiler, R. E., Hicks, A. P. and Hicks, M. R. (1995) 'The multi-modal diagnosis and treatment of Attention Deficit Hyperactivity Disorder', *Therapeutic Care and Education*, 4 (2), 4–9

Dewey, J. (1933) *How we Think*, Boston MA: DC Heath

DfEE (2001) *Promoting Children's Mental Health with Early Years and School Settings*, Nottingham: DfEE Publications

Dunn, R. and Dunn, K. (1993a) *Teaching Elementary Students through their Individual Learning Styles: Practical Approaches for Grades 3–6*, Boston: Allyn and Bacon

Dunn, R. and Dunn, K. (1993b) *Teaching Secondary Students through their Individual Learning Styles: Practical Approaches for Grades 7–12*, Boston, MA: Allyn and Bacon

Dutton, G. (1997) 'Visual problems in children with brain damage', in *Approaches to Working with Children with Multiple Disabilities and a Visual Impairment*, London: on behalf of Vital by RNIB

Dutton, K. (1989) *Writing under Examination Conditions*, Glasgow: Scottish Education Department Regional Psychological Service

Dyslexia in the Primary Classroom (1997) Teaching Today series, London: BBC Education in association with British Dyslexia Association

Ennis, R. H. (1987) 'A taxonomy of critical thinking dispositions and abilities', in J. Baron and R. Sternberg (eds) *Teaching for Thinking*, New York: Freeman

Frey, K. S. and Ruble, D. N. (1985) 'What children say when the teacher is not around: conflicting goals in social comparison and performance assessment in the classroom', *Journal of Personality and Social Psychology*, 48, 550–62

Frith, U. (1985) 'Beneath the surface of developmental dyslexia', in K. E. Patterson, M. Coltheart and J. Marshall (eds) *Surface Dyslexia*, London: LEA

Furman, W., Rahe, D. F. and Hartup, W. W. (1979) 'Rehabilitation of socially withdrawn pre-school children through mixed-age and same-age socialization', *Child Development*, 50, 915–22

Gibbs, G. (1988) *Learning by Doing: A Guide to Teaching and Learning Methods*, Birmingham: SCED

Goleman, D. (1996) *Emotional Intelligence*, London: Bloomsbury

Gray, C. (1994) *The Social Story Book*, Arlington VA: Future Horizons

Hall, D. (1995) *Assessing the Needs of Bilingual Pupils: Living in Two Languages*, London: David Fulton

Hardwick, J. (1996) 'Irregular little beasties', *Special Children*, June–July, 7–10

Harris, J. R. (1997) *The Nurture Assumption*, London: Bloomsbury

Harter, S. (1982) 'The perceived competence scale for children', *Child Development*, 53, 87–97

Hayes, N. (1984) *A First Course in Psychology*, Walton on Thames: Nelson

Hewett, D. (ed.) (2000) *Challenging Behaviour: Principles and Practices*, London: David Fulton

Hoffman, M. L. (1982) 'Development of prosocial motivation: empathy and guilt', in N. Eisenberg (ed.) *The Development of Prosocial Behaviour*, New York: Academic Press

Howlin, P., Baron-Cohen, S. and Hadwin, J. (1999) *Teaching Children with Autism to Mind-read: A Practical Guide*, Chichester: Wiley

Kagan, S. (1988) *Cooperative Learning: Resources for Teacher*, Riverside CA: University of California Press

Koshy, V., Ernest, P. and Casey, R. (2000) *Mathematics for Primary Teachers*, London: Routledge

Kwa, L. (1994) 'Adolescent females' perceptions of competence: what is defined as healthy and achieving', in J. Gallivan, S. D. Crozier and V. M. Lalande (eds) *Women, Girls, and Achievement*, North York, Ontario: Captus University Publications

Lawrence, D. (1996) *Enhancing Self-esteem in the Classroom*, London: Paul Chapman

Leadbetter, J., Morris, S., Timmins, P., Knight, G. and Traxson, D. (1999) *Applying Psychology in the Classroom*, London: David Fulton

Long, M. (2000) *The Psychology of Education*, London: RoutledgeFalmer

Mannarino, A. P. (1980) 'The development of children's friendships', in H. C. Foot, A. J. Chapman and J. R. Smith (eds) *Friendship and Social Relations in Children*, Chichester: Wiley

McLinden, M. and Hendrickson, H. (1998) 'Using tactile symbols: a review of current issues', in *Approaches to Working with Children with Multiple Disabilities and a Visual Impairment*, London: RNIB for Vital

Mead, G. H. (1934) *Mind, Self and Society*, Chicago: University of Chicago Press

Mesibov, G. (2003) *What is TEACCH* www.teacch.com/ (27 March 2003)

Miller, P. H. (1990) 'The development of strategies of selective attention', in D. F. Bjorklund (ed.) *Children's Strategies: Contemporary Views of Cognitive Development*, Hillsdale NJ: Erlbaum

Moffatt, E. (2001) 'Writing social stories to improve students' social understanding, *GAP*, 2 (1), 12–14

Moon, J. A. (1999) *Reflection in Learning and Professional Development*, London: Kogan Page

National Deaf Children's Society (2001) *Understanding Deafness*, London: NDCS Publications

National Oracy Project (1990) *Teaching, Talking and Learning in Key Stage One*, York: NCC

Nelson-Jones, R. (1993) *Practical Counselling and Helping Skills*, 3rd edn, London: Cassell

O'Connor, R. D. (1972) 'Relative efficacy of modelling, shaping and the combined procedures for modification of social withdrawal', *Journal of Abnormal Psychology*, 79, 327–34

Ockelford, A. (1998) 'Making sense of the world', in *Approaches to Working with Children with Multiple Disabilities and a Visual Impairment*, London: on behalf of Vital by RNIB

Oden, S. and Asher, S. R. (1977) 'Coaching children in social skills for friendship making', *Child Development*, 48, 495–506

Ornstein, P. A., Naus, M. J., and Liberty, C. (1975) 'Rehearsal and organisational processes in children's memory', *Child Development*, 46, 818–30

Parker, J. G. and Asher, S. R. (1987) 'Peer relations and later personal adjustment: are low-accepted children at risk?' *Psychological Bulletin*, 102, 357–89

Pascal, L. (2002) *The Dyslexic in the Classroom, Special Needs* London: Publishers' Association

Pickard, J. (1999) 'Sense and sensitivity', *People Management*, 28 October, 48–56

Riley, J. (1999) *Teaching Reading at Key Stage 1 and Before*, Cheltenham: Stanley Thornes

Ripley, K., Daines, B. and Barrett, J. (1997) *Dyspraxia: A Guide for Teachers and Parents*, London: David Fulton

Robinson, F. P. (1970) *Effective Study*, 4th edn, New York: Harper and Row

Rose, C. (1987) *Accelerated Learning*, Aylesbury: Accelerated Learning Systems

Rosenthal, R. and Jacobson, L. (1966) 'Teachers' expectancies: determinants of pupils' IQ gains', *Psychological Reports*, 19, 115–18

Rowe, C. (1999) 'Do social stories benefit children with autism in mainstream primary school?' *British Journal of Special Education*, 26 (1), 12–14

Sadker, M. and Sadker, D. (1994) *Failing at Fairness: How America's Schools Cheat Girls*, New York: Scribner's

Schachter, F. F. and Strage, A. A. (1982) 'Adults' talk and children's language development', in S. G. Moore and C. R. Cooper (eds) *The Young Child: Reviews of Research* III, Washington DC: National Association for the Education of Young Children

Selman, R. L. and Jaquette, D. (1977) 'Stability and oscillation in interpersonal awareness a clinical-developmental analysis', in C. B. Keasey (ed.) *The Nebraska Symposium on Motivation*, XXV, Lincoln NE: University of Nebraska Press

Shevin, M. and Klein, N. K. (1984) 'The importance of choice-making skills for students with severe disabilities', *The Association for Persons with Severe Handicaps*, 9 (3), 159–66

Sigelman, C. K. and Shaffer, D. R. (1991) *Life-span Human Development*, Monterey CA: Brooks Cole

Smith, C. (2001) 'Using social stories with children with autistic spectrum disorders: an evaluation', *GAP*, 2 (1), 16–25

Smith, P. K., Cowie, H. and Blades, M. (1998) *Understanding Children's Development*, 3rd edn, Oxford: Blackwell

Snow, C. (1977) 'The development of conversation between mothers and babies', *Journal of Child Language*, 4, 1–22

Snow, C. E., and Ferguson, C. A. (eds) (1977) *Talking to Children*, Cambridge: Cambridge University Press

Special Children (2000a) 'Dyspraxia – at a glance', *Special Children*, 129, May, 22

Special Children (2000b) 'ADHD – at a glance', *Special Children*, 130, June–
July, 36

Special Children (2000c) 'Dyslexia – at a glance', *Special Children*, 132, October,
28

Special Children (2001a) 'Down's syndrome – at a glance', *Special Children*, 134,
January, 33

Special Children (2001b) 'Autistic spectrum disorder – at a glance', *Special
Children*, 136, March, 37

Thomson, M. (1990) *Developmental Dyslexia*, 3rd edn, London: Whurr

Tuckman, B. and Jensen, N. (1977) 'Stages of small group development revisited', *Group and Organizational Studies*, 2, 419–27

Watson, C. (1995) 'Helping families from other cultures decide on how to
talk to their child with language delay', *Wig Wag*, winter, 95

Wragg, E. C. and Brown, G. (1993) *Explaining in the Primary School*, London:
Routledge

Index